Hardwicke Drummond Rawnsley

Valete, Tennyson

And Other Memorial Poems

Hardwicke Drummond Rawnsley

Valete, Tennyson
And Other Memorial Poems

ISBN/EAN: 9783744712248

Printed in Europe, USA, Canada, Australia, Japan

Cover: Foto ©Thomas Meinert / pixelio.de

More available books at **www.hansebooks.com**

Tennyson
and other
Memorial
Poems
by
H. D. Rawnsley

DEDICATED

ALFRED LORD TENNYSON
Poet Laureate

CONTENTS.

𝔗ennyson.

The Royal Dead.

Heroes among Men.

Leaders of Men.

Shepherds of Men.

CONTENTS.

Singers among Men.

Thinkers among Men.

Friends and Neighbours.

CONTENTS.

A. F.

CONTENTS.

Dedicatory.

You, where the hills are uprolled
  Grey from the yellowing fen,
Found dim glory of old,
  Left it bright among men.
Child of the stream and the glen,
  Singer of weald and of wold,
Take this gift from a pen
  That in praise of the Poet is bold.

TENNYSON.

Obiit October 6, 1892.

Tennyson.

OBIIT, ALDWORTH, OCTOBER 6TH, 1892.

THE moonlight lay with glory on his face
  About whose bed in grief the nation bowed,
  And darkly flew the wild October cloud :
Sobbed the pale morn, and came with faltering pace
  As if it feared to lift a dead man's shroud;
  And all the streams made lamentation loud.

But such majestic calm was in his look
  As seemed to say, 'Why weeping o'er me bend,
  Or bid me longer here on earth attend
Whose home is Heaven?' His hand held Shake-
    speare's book—
  Shakespeare, so soon to greet him as a friend !
  And so he went companioned, to the end.

Then to the poet, crowned with power and years,

  One bore the wreath of immortality,

  And laid his chaplet of green laurel by.

Wept England; over-seas a land in tears

  For its own bard,[1] caught up the bitter cry

  That rings right round the world when singers die.

For he, the music-maker of the earth,

  Who ruled of right by sound's melodious sway,

  Who still within his heart had words to say,

Turned to the home whence all his song had birth;

  The first, last, Laureate of a golden day,

  Untouched by time, passed painlessly away.

But as men sorrowed for the glory gone,

  And the dark dumbness fallen upon the time,

  There rang from Heaven triumphant angel-chime,

And voices cried, " Behold the twain are one,

  The friend beloved, who left him ere his prime,

  The friend who made Love's great Memorial Rhyme."

[1] Whittier.

And lo! at ending of that heavenly psalm

   The silent sunshine flooded all the lea,

   The golden leaf scarce fluttered from the tree,

The distant ocean lay in autumn-calm;

   There was "no moaning at the bar," when he—

   Our princely poet-soul, put out to sea.

But we are left disconsolate; no lyre

   To sound a people's glory, soothe its pain,

   No trumpet-call to chivalry again,

No words of subtlest feeling, finest fire

   To keep us still a nation, and no strain

   To bring new Knowledge to a wiser reign.

He was true patriot, and his soul was set

   To give our England flowers of song for weeds.

   He planted well, he scattered fruitful seeds;

He showed us love was more than coronet,

   And in the jarring of a hundred creeds

   Taught life and truth were hid in noble deeds.

Yet most that purest passion for a maid
  And manly love with maiden virtue crowned,
  Availed to keep our social fabric sound;
And loving Arthur well, he well pourtrayed
  That kingliest Arthur of the Table Round,
  Who entered Heaven to heal him of Earth's wound.

And he has entered Heaven by earth unharmed;
  Years could not blanch a single lock with grey,
  Time could not steal a single bolt away,
Nor blunt the sword wherewith his soul was armed:
  But from this shore, whereon he might not stay,
  His music nevermore shall die away.

Now he is gone, who up the windy ways
  Followed the shepherd to the bleating fold;
  Who, when the level plain was laid in gold,
Ran with the reapers, learnt their Doric phrase,
  And to his great iambic's stately mould
  Caught back rich words that never can grow old.

Now he is gone, who spoke with Greece and Rome,
And took the herdsman's sunny pipe, and played
Idyllic music fit for English shade;
Who in his ocean-sounding island home
Walked with the mighty Homer unafraid,
And Saxon metre to his thunder made.

I shall not find his welcome at the home,
Nor front those searching eyes that when we met
Would ask what father's-features lingered yet;
Nor mark the sun-browned ample forehead's dome,
Strong Norman mouth-swirls, cheeks whereon was set
The powerful seal of the Plantagenet.

I shall not press that soft and tender hand,
Nor hear far off his rich voice like a bell
Ring after crying "Friend! farewell, farewell!"
Nor see the dreaming dark-cloaked poet stand
Like some Velasquez figure in the dell,
Where o'er his face full shadow rose and fell.

Friends! we no more shall climb the darkened down

    And hear him measure music to the beat

    Of summer seas reverberant at his feet;

Never in orchard-garden overblown

    With spice of rose and lily, and made sweet

    With song of birds, can share his arbour seat,

And listen to the tale of boyhood days

    Not quite forgotten, in the Lincoln land

    Of corn that yellowed to the yellow sand,

Where first he strove to win a mother's praise

    By warbling with his brother, hand in hand,

    The wild-wood notes her heart could understand,

Or move from boyhood's day and personal theme

    To hint of curious workmanship confessed

    In some great thought his labour had expressed,

To talk of nations, and the poet's dream

    Of England, free, pure, faithful, self-possessed,

    His fears for Modred's battle in the West.

With him we cannot claim the moorland walk

   And watch the sunlight shoot athwart the rain,

   Or halt to hear new bird-notes in the lane;

Or see him stoop from philosophic talk

   To shred some simple wayside weed in twain,

   And marvel at the miracle made plain.

Nor ever view soft veils of vapour drawn

   From the 'grey sea' beyond the Sussex glade,

   Nor watch from Aldworth's height, the morning made,

Nor ever leave the cedar-scented lawn

   To thread the high-o'er-arching colonnade

   Of cloistral trees that gave the poet shade.

And when the birds have sought their ilex home,

   And the magnolia pours its fragrance rare,

   We shall not mount again his turret stair

And hear the strong deep-chested music come,

   While light in hand within his simple chair

   He summoned sound to people all the air,

And set the rafters ringing to the wail

    Of a great nation for its warrior dead,

    The boom of cannon and the mourner's tread;

Or bade the bugle's elfin echoes fail,

    The long low lights on castle walls be shed—

    Then shut the book in dream, and bowed his head.

Nor ever after meat when lamps are lit,

    About the shining table drawing nigher,

    Feel the fine soul that flashed forth at desire;

Sharp sallies, rapier-thrusts of genial wit

    That called for friend, and bade the foe retire,

    And filled the hall with laughter, and with fire.

The hall is filled with silence and with tears!

    The stately hound that licked his dying hand,

    Fair-flewed, rough-chested, sorrowful must stand,

Must wonder why no well-loved step he hears,

    Or, restless, roam among the funeral band

    That comes to bear his master thro' the land.

Yea ! bear him down, by weald, and wood, and town ;

He knew each rosy farm, he loved each lane,

For he was home-bred English.   Lo ! the plain

Is gold from harvest ; he, whom Death has mown

In ripeness, goes to where our goodliest grain

Is garnered, till the Christ return again.

Bear him in some triumphal leafy car,

Laced round with moss, with laurel interwove,

And let the simple pall be strewn above

With all white flowers that pure and fragrant are—

Wild roses, on the pall embroidered, prove

His zeal for knightliness, our England's love.

But bear him when the sunset, saffron-gold,

Floods the pale Heaven, above the moorland height,

And in the west one waning star hangs bright ;

For now the race is run, the tale is told,

One last lone star sinks down into the night,

Our one last prophet vanishes from sight.

For, though I find thy voice in hall or cot,

    And see thy words in every flying sheet,

    Or hear thee lisped by children in the street,

And murmured in the cloister,—Thou art not.

    Thy soul, that shunned earth's restlessness and
        heat,

    Has sought Heaven's unapproachable retreat.

I trace the brooklet swirling to the plain

    From near the copse beside thy father's door,

    That ancient grove whence 'holy waters' pour;[1]

I pass by thorpe and tower toward the main,

    I roam the long sands thou didst love of yore,[2]

    But ah! thy feet have left the lonely shore.

Far off, by Cam, I catch the careless chimes,[3]

    Through close-cropt meads and stately halls I
        stray,

[1] Holywell Wood, at Somersby, Lincolnshire.
[2] Skegness, Lincolnshire.
[3] The Lime Walk, Trinity College, Cambridge, 1828-1831.

Where those disciples of thy glorious day [1]

Made mirth and music underneath the limes,

Thou with the twelve—nigh latest didst thou stay;

But now the last leaf falls, the world is grey.

I wander to the chapel by the mere,

I win the Hall, beyond the grove of pine,[2]

Where-over, Skiddaw doth at day's decline

Shed back its fern-flushed glory. Thou wert there—

There didst out-roll 'Morte d'Arthur' line on line

To willing ears—thy ghost alone is mine.

Or leaving Thames I seek by chalky dell [3]

My father's terrace-garden o'er the flood,

Where once a bride and bridegroom-poet stood,

And heard in June-tide air the marriage bell

Ring thro' the walnuts that "the hour is good

When noble man weds noblest woman-hood."

[1] See Note 1.
[2] Mirehouse, Home of the Speddings, 1835.
[3] Shiplake-on-Thames, where Tennyson was married, 1850.

There now perchance in thought slow moveth one

    Pale and in pain : she hears another sound,

    Her eyes for sorrow cannot leave the ground,

The gentlest wife that ever bore a son,

    Who once for Love and Life, went gaily-gowned,

    And now, for Death, with weeds is wrapt around.

Then to the church close-bosomed in the chine,[1]

    Where moves and moans the silver Severn sea,

    I turn.   I feel thy spirit, joyous, free ;

There lies the heart, once lost, now wholly thine,

    Of whose true wards thy music held the key ;

    There men who mourn shall surely meet with

    thee.

[1] Clevedon, 31st Jan., 1834.

Somersby.

HERE was the haunt of those three nightingales,
   Whose voices soothed an England of unrest
Thro' changeful seasons. From the circling crest
Of yonder hill they saw the far-off sails
Shine as great Hingvar's shone. The viking tales
   Of that fierce worm that all the wold possest
   Rang in their ears, and knights that dared their best
Knelt in near churches clad with chain and scales.

And here they mixed with peasants, learned the lore
   Of peaceful men who tend the flock and wain,
   Here, book in hand, they wandered thro' the grove,
   But most they loved beside the beck to rove,
The brook that murmured prose toward the plain,
But, since they sang, sings on for evermore.

See Note 2.

Clevedon.

HE missed the fresh, salt, eastern airs that blow,
　　The mills that whirl their white arms in the wind;
　　His father's ashes he had left, to find
Love's heart inurned where Severn's waters flow.
Here in the marsh the hollow reeds might grow
　　For sound to suit the sorrow of his mind;
　　But grief needs friendly ears to keep it kind,
And his beloved unheeding lies below.

Then to sad eyes thy cottage gave reproof—
　　Thy cottage, Coleridge, by the western sea,
　　　Its simple chimneys and its gable-end;
For he remembered there his chamber-roof,
　　Hid in the poplar shade of Somersby!
　　　And the lone poet found in thee a friend.

See Note 3.

𝕱arringforð.

1883.

THIS is the Poets home, from east to west
  A silver amulet, the Solent shines,
  To guard him, where he sees in stately lines
The white-winged vessels pass, for toil or rest.
No ruder sound has his fine ear distrest
  Than rippling ilex, and the sigh of pines
  When south winds sweep with clamour up the chines,
And waves leap high on milk-white Watcomb's breast.

But if at all he leave his song's retreat,
  The cypress bowers, the labyrinthine maze,
  To climb the hushed, companionable Down,
  And seaward at the Beacon's height to gaze,
He hears the ocean like his great heart beat,
  And to its rhythmic cadence times his own.

On Leaving Farringford.

1883.

YOU waved your hand, I could not say farewell,
    For those last words, " My time can not be long,"
Took speech away. Great Leader of our song,
Time cannot touch the thought-built citadel
Wherein thou sittest throned ! What sovereign spell,
    If thy voice ceases, what prevailing tongue,
    Can tune earth's discords, show us right from wrong
And light the darkening years wherein we dwell ?

But if the dread, inevitable hour
    Comes near, and now the music of thy mind
      Is fit for angels' high intelligence,
    Yet take thy harp, leave one last strain behind,
To bid us guide the world's advancing power
    Up steps of change, with slow-foot reverence.

To Alfred, Lord Tennyson.

JANUARY 18TH, 1884.

NEW Lord of England, but old lord of song,
    Voice to the realm, in council of our peers
    Long present, peerless, for these many years
Thy muse in her nobility was strong
To sit high-throned above earth's common throng,
    Thy helm such laurels as a poet wears,
    Thy sword a pen that knew not any fears,
Weapon for lordly right against the wrong.

And if no children's children in thy hall,
    Pointing to broken lance and battered shield,
        Shall say, "These arms the first great Baron wore!"
    Thy verse, that fired our deeds by flood and field,
        That gave us back the chivalry of yore,
Will sound like clarions on our country's wall.

To Lord Tennyson.

ON HIS 80TH BIRTHDAY, AUGUST 6TH, 1889.

THE four-score years that blanch the heads of men
　　Touch not the immortals, and we bring to-day
　No flowers to twine with laurel and with bay,
Seeing the spring is with thee now, as when
Above the wold and marsh and mellowing fen
　　Thy song bade England listen.　Powers decay,
　　Hands fail, and eyes, tongues scarce their will
　　can say,
But still Heaven's fire burns in thy hollow pen.

Oh, singer of the knightly days of old!
　Oh, ringer of the knell to lust and hate!
　　Oh, bringer of new hope from memory's shrine!
When God doth set in Heaven thy harp of gold,
　The souls that made this generation great
　　Shall own, The voice that nerved their hearts
　　was thine.

𝔄 Storp from the "𝔄rabian 𝔑ights."

1889.

T^O one, a Chief Physician in the land,
Nasr-ed-Din the Persian, King of Kings,
Sends greeting; bids when dawn to-morrow brings,
The great Hhâkeem shall kneel to kiss his hand.
To whom the Chief Physician: "Sire, command
Aught else, to-morrow's haste with plumy wings
Bears me to one, our Laureate Lord, who sings
For in his presence I am sworn to stand."

Whereat waxed wroth the Shah; then spake his page:—
"Nay! hath not music mightier realms than thine?
The singer's rule about the world doth run,
The Bard is King of Kings by right divine."
"Well spoken, boy, give the Hhâkeem his wage,
Salute him, Knight of Lion and of Sun."

See Note 4.

A Farewell to the "Sunbeam."

1889.

WE watched the ship from speck to phantom grow,
    From phantom to its three fair towers of sail,
    Then o'er the Solent's tide of silver pale
We saw the sunset flash upon thy bow.
The whole air sang, waves sang as we did row,
    We heard from land the far-off nightingale,
    But clear above all music an "All hail!"
Broke o'er us as we neared the golden prow.

Farewell! no Syrens shall thy keel perplex,
    No need of thongs thy pilot safe to bind
        From death in Scylla's song-enchanted seas;
        For one full-voiced as old Mæonides
And skilled as Orpheus, walks the shining decks,
    Whose spell shall charm the deeps and woo the wind.

On hearing Lord Tennyson read his Ode on
the Death of the Duke of Wellington.

GREAT builder of this monument of sound
    To him whose praise shall never cease to be,
    As long as hearts beat fast for victory,
Or laurels grow on any English ground!—
Oh! how my heart and how mine ears were bound,
    Hearing the boom of that articulate sea
    Which, wave on wave of wondrous melody,
Flowed in from deeps of gratefulness profound!

The sands may chafe old Chephren's pyramid,
    The Colosseum crumble and decay,
        Yea, even the Dome that shows the golden cross
        Sink with its whisper of a nation's loss—
And the world-victor's victor's tomb be hid—
    But this sonorous cenotaph shall stay.

After the Epilogue to the Charge of the Heavy Brigade.

WHEN thrushes called between the day and
  night,
  And you clomb up the down toward the stars,
  My heart went with you, for the thoughtful bars
Of that last music had possessed me quite.
True seer, I cried, you have delivered right
  The only message that, to heal our scars,
  Unriddling these dread necessary wars,
Can crown with song the soldier's deed of might.

For till these bastions crumble with the frost,
  Or earth shall meet the sun and melt in fire,
    Some new-won land shall court the jealous eye,
    Some voice shall startle lust and tyranny,
Some heart refuse to own the battle lost,
  Some patriot find in death his soul's desire.

𝔇eath and 𝔉ame.

1890.

FROM Lym to Yar I crossed the Solent flood,
   And sought the village nestling 'neath the Down
   Where you, whom more than four-score summers
      crown,
Sing from the solemn shelter of your wood.
Once more beside your cedar-tree I stood,
   Climbed the grey ridge, and saw the distance frown
   And flash to silver, heard the long wave thrown
In music on your island solitude.

We talked of those old foemen, Death and Fame,
And you, you told me how a letter came
   Wherein a young girl summoned heart to say—
"Tell him I read his poems, and I rise
Ever with will to be more good, more wise."
   You sighed, Death vanished, only Fame could stay.

"𝔈 𝔥𝔞𝔟𝔢 𝔒𝔭𝔢𝔫𝔢𝔡 𝔱𝔥𝔢 𝔅𝔬𝔬𝔨."

AT ALDWORTH, OCTOBER 5TH, 1892.

YEA, thou hast opened book on book, who now,
  While the mist gathers ere the light breaks in,
  Dost open this. For from thy books we win
How life and love lead upward, blest but slow;
How knowledge humbleth, lifting up the low;
    How Reverence is of Heaven; Pride,—earth and sin;
    How self is weakness, to the brute akin,
And self-restraint such strength as angels know.

And thou hast opened now that other Book
  Whereof through life, with longings manifold,
    Thy soul did yearn: therein thou readest clear
    The names of friend and son, so lost, so dear;
Yea, and therein all living ones that look
  Shall find thine own, immortal, writ in gold.

                                    See Note 5.

The Poet's Death-Chamber.

OCTOBER 6TH, 1892.

"There were no lights in the room, but the moon's rays streamed in through the oriel window, and lighted up the face and form of the dying Poet."

NOT in the bright, unsolitary noon,

When all the air with life and music rings,

Came the great hush of those archangel wings,

That gave the singer peace and endless boon;

But rather at the midnight hour of swoon

When Sleep, Death's prophet, unto nature brings

Surcease of sense and outward communings

Beneath that world of loneliness the moon.

And so he grew to marble—he who made

In hearts of stone the generous life-blood run,

But o'er him dead, Death's planet wheeling slow

Flung down such splendour through the awful shade,

As bade us feel his soul was with the Sun

And needed Death to give us back the glow.

The Laureate Dead.

OCTOBER 6TH, 1892.

THE laurels fall from off as high a brow
    As since our Shakespeare wore the poet-bays;
    Who breathed Sicilian music thro' his lays,
And felt great Homer's resonant ebb and flow,
Who knew all art of word that man may know,
    And led us on by love's undying ways,
    Who gave us back the old Arthurian days,
Latest of Laureates, Tennyson, lies low.

Our golden age is shorter, and the spheres
    That sooner wane may swiftlier wax to prime,
        But when shall sing another as he sung,
        Who wrought with Saxon purity of tongue
The one great Epic of two hundred years,
    The one Memorial utterance for all time?

Tennyson's Home-Going.

BEAR him by quiet wood and silent down,
    And let the first gold leafage on him fall,
His leaf of Life fell golden.   Let the pall
Be strewn with English roses, and the crown
Of gold and laurel on his bier be shown.
    For now the laurel fades beyond recall
    The rose of song lies shattered; in the hall
Of Heaven, he wears that wreath he made his own.

Yea! bear him from the fair fields of his love
    To that old abbey of the Faithful King;
        The roaring streets, that felt thro' all their roar
        His psalm of peace, shall never wake him more;
And leave him there where Chaucer's heart shall move
    For joy to greet the brother whom ye bring.

Leabing Albworth.

OCTOBER 11TH, 1892.

WHEN from his laurel grove, reluctant, slow,
  To his far rest we bore the Poet dead,
One star alone in Heaven its radiance shed,
So lingered long our sad day's after-glow;
But when we neared that twilit town below,
  A thousand stars our mute procession led:
  The "Lyre" shone bright, the "Swan" flew overhead
And high on Hindhead, level stood the "Plow."

A thousand suns that from the dawn had gleamed
  Above his sleep, but waited eventide
    To show their lamps and light the Poet home:
A thousand worlds from which full glory streamed,
    To give us hope that though the dark had come,
  His star of song should brighten and abide.

The Two Poets.

" **A**DMIRINGLY, affectionately yours,"
    So wrote his brother bard upon the day
    When eighty years of life had rolled away
And blessed us from the stream that still outpours
Of harmony for England's harsher hours.
    " That I have loved you dearly let this say,
    Secure your glorious song on earth will stay
When your high soul shall seek the Heavenly bowers."

Now his high soul has won the heavenly place,
    He who from out cool shadow saw the heat
        Of earth's endeavour, sees from sunnier height
The covering cast on all the nation's face,
    And, from his unassailable ‑retreat,
        He feels far off ' our wonder, our delight.'

See Note 6.

Christmas without the Laureate.

1892.

THE organ peals, the white-robed chorus tells,
    That tale the shepherds heard their flocks among,

When open wide the gates of Heaven were flung,

Where Bethlehem's village from her plain upswells.

Yet ah! one voice has failed! Our old church bells

    Give back an echo of the songs he sung,

    But sadness sounds in every silver tongue

That sends this Christmas message up the Fells.

For he who knew indeed the Word was God,

    Who felt the Faith that sought the Holy Grail,

    Who set a lamp of Duty in the mist,

Who smote the beast in man with iron rod,

    And sang two generations back to Christ,

        Sings now more sweetly—but behind the veil.

Charles Tennyson Turner.

APRIL 25, 1879.

MAKER of songs most simple and most sweet,
With artlessness that only art commands,
Thy notes are hushed, the lute has slipped thy hands,
And lies still echoing with thy heart's last beat,
Full tuned and fit for service, at thy feet.
But whoso dares to wake its tender strands
Must know the touch a humble soul demands,
And eyes of love that lowliest things will greet.

In thee the dumb creation found a voice;
Though fenced and fine thy music's dainty sphere,
No wings that flashed but did thy song rejoice,
No hedge-row cry but found a listening ear;
Child-hearted thou, by nature as by choice,
True Christian Poet! blameless Sonneteer!

C

At Mablethorpe;

AN EPISODE IN THE PUBLICATION OF THE " POEMS BY
TWO BROTHERS." 1827.

THAT evening's sun set rosy o'er the wold,
A burnished shield the level marsh-land lay;
Tall reeds in wonder whispered all the way
As towards the sea their car of triumph rolled;
The whirling mills with voices manifold
Tossed up their arms to cheer; the churches grey—
The lonely churches where the marsh-men pray—
Breathed forth a blessing on the venture bold.

Thou far retiring ocean, o'er what sands
Of rippled silver glistening to the stars
Didst thou entice those happy brothers' feet;
With what a rhythm didst thou clap thy hands,
And rear thyself above the shelving bars,
And pause, and fall, their music to repeat!

See Note 7.

To a Portrait of the Mother of the Poets.

GRASBY VICARAGE, 1873.

SWEET mother of the many nightingales,
    Who in a northern land that seldom heard
The passionate warbling of the Attic bird,
Poured out on Lincoln wolds and Lincoln dales
Such song as never with the season fails,
    In Spring, or when the wheat to shade is stirred,
    Or when by wintry winds the mills are whirred,
Or breathless Autumn stays their shining sails.

Sweet mother of that swarthy brotherhood,
    Tho' all the world should swear their southern race,
    And one still sings of those far Grecian isles,
    The wilding rose that in thy bosom smiles,
No surelier drew from English earth its blood
    To fill our English June with joy and grace.

THE ROYAL DEAD.

𝔈𝔫 𝔱𝔥𝔢 ℭ𝔥𝔲𝔯𝔠𝔥 𝔬𝔣 𝔖𝔱. 𝔊𝔢𝔬𝔯𝔤𝔢.

(BUILT IN MEMORY OF II.R.II. PRINCE LEOPOLD, DIED AT
CANNES, MARCII 28TII, 1884.)

GUARD well, St. George, our prince's memory,
   High-o'er the lustrous pines and sunny bowers,
   When dawn climbs up the wave, or when the towers
Of ancient Cannes stand dark against the sea;
And let the weird self-healing olive tree,
   Emblem of Life, beyond Death's harmful powers,
   Grow round the house of Prayer, and orange flowers
With soft mimosa clouds for incense be.

And since his young life's rose, that knew no blame,
   Fell here, tho' nursed upon our English shore,
      Let the wild woodland rose that blooms for all
   Gleam in the rich mosaic evermore,
      And every evening's sun make roses fall
Upon the shrine that keeps his honoured name.

See Note 8.

The Emperor William I.

ON HIS 90TH BIRTHDAY.

KAISER, and crowned with ninety summers now,
　　If every stream that babbled to the Rhine
　　Spake human speech, to-day its praise were thine.
Ageless of heart and zeal—oak-natured thou,
Come forth and let the wondering nations know
　　How kings may still be kings by power divine,
　　How monarch's might can people's right enshrine,
And patriot love to royal wisdom bow.

Great worker with the tireless brain and hand,
　　Head winter-white—Soul Spring with fullest powers,
　　Unhurt by praise and never warped by blame,
　　Heaven waits thee, King, but Earth shall keep
　　　　thy name,
　　Ours now, when God shall call thee hence still ours,
By all that made and keeps us Fatherland.

The Dying Kaiser.

MARCH 8TH, 1888.

KAISER, with thrice the tale of royal years
    That made the new-found Alexander great,
    At length thou nearest the mysterious gate
To mingle with the kings of old—thy peers—
And find few mightier. Lo! thy forehead wears
    A crown, whence, even in heaven, will scintillate
    The rainbow lights of love; thy cloak of state
Is jewelled with a nation's loyal tears.

But when the dread rememberable day
    Shall call thee from the kingdom thou hast made
        To that high court, where kings as subjects
        stand,
At least the vows we vow, the prayers we pray,
    Shall go before through silence and the shade,
        And give thee welcome home to Fatherland!

The Kaiser at Peace.

MARCH 9TII, 1888.

NOW let the Rhine flow sad by tower and lea,
    And all the Teuton woods a requiem sing,
    Lo! he who made the nation, warrior king,
Bows at the last to death's august decree:
Great freedom-giver, he himself is free;
    Freed from the care that crowns shall ever bring,
    From weary watch upon the foemen-ring,
From love's last yearning towards the southern sea.

Oh! by the grim Sadowa and Sedan
    And those dark violets crushed before his car,
        The day faint Paris yielded all but pride,
    Weep for a Kaiser, glorious in war,
Warder of home, and Leader in the van
        Of Peace: for peace he toiled, in peace he died.

A Brave Empress.

QUEEN of the weary days and watchful nights,
　　While all our Europe, bowed about the bed,
　　Implored the Great Upbringer from the dead
To bring thy Prince and crown him on the heights
Of health—the bravest in his country's fights—
　　Simplest of men the purple ever bred,
　　And most unflinching—though above his head
Death, with a cold dark crown, proclaimed its rights.

We knew your worth, for we had known your choice;
　　We had not felt what courage love could bring,
　　Until we saw the burghers at your feet
Stand silent for their grief, and heard your voice,
　　Clear, where their voices failed for tears, repeat
A people's sorrow for their sorrowing king.

See Note 9.

The Crown of Thorns.

HIGH on the altar lay the cirque of gold,
　The heavy crown of kingliness and care,
　And he reached out to take it, but the air
Was thick with doubt, and voices manifold
Forewarning, "Sire, thine arms are over bold!"
　Then, as his hands sank crownless, he was ware
　Of Christ's face, pale and pitiful, in His hair
He saw the thorns they crowned Him with of old.

And at that sign of Christ, so crowned with pain,
　So lonely in the sorrow of a King,
　　So kingly in His sorrow's loneliness,
　　He felt the strength that could upbear the
　　　stress
　Of all the pain his crown of thorns would bring,
And dared to claim the kingship and to reign.

See Note 10.

Mourners Absent from the Kaiser's Funeral.

MARCH 16TH, 1888.

PRINCE of the head to think, the soul to feel,
  The will to govern, and the hand to guide,
  With that twin pillar-statesman at your side,
Who built the nation's wall of guardian steel—
For you we grieve the most. Dark death must heal
  The wound Death gave, and lonely in the tide
  You still must stand rock-natured, and must hide
A heart that aches for him who gave the Seal.

But when the torches flamed upon the way—
  That sad triumphal way—and cannons' boom
    Shook the drear streets walled up to bitter heaven
With signs of woe and faces in dismay,
    We thanked our God such friends to kings
      were given,
    Our praises filled the absent mourners' room.

See Note 11.

The Letter of Frederick III. to Prince Bismarck.

" NOT caring for the splendour of great deeds
        And strife for glory, but with this content
    That some day graven on my monument
    The humblest child of Fatherland may read,
    ' He who the glorious Kaiser did succeed
        Was sworn to Peace—his rule beneficent,
        He served his people, on their welfare bent
    And sowed for generations hence Faith's seed.' "

Oh, by the palms and laurels 'neath the dome
    Where rests before the dark-draped altar shrine
        The warrior king who made a nation one,
        Did father e'er beget a nobler son ?
Had ever people, when their chief went home
    A surer pledge of kingliness divine ?

The Emperor Frederick.

JUNE 15TH, 1888.

WHEN Europe wept and over east and west
    Hung sorrow for the Kaiser gone before,
  We prayed that life would seal Death's awful door
And give us back our bravest and our best,
King in his father's room ; but that dark guest
  Clung to his side, slow poisoned at the core
  The heart that cared for all his country's poor,
Thought royal deeds, but never thought of rest.

Two moons had filled and when the third had waned,
  O'ershadowed by the weary travelling earth,
    He bowed a head that never yet had owned
  Flesh mortal, so he passed; but praise had birth,
    Honour for him whom noble suffering crowned,
Love for a King who in Death's court had reigned.

Frederick III.

1888.

K ING for a hundred days, a hundred years
    Shall not undo the greatness of thy reign,
    Lord of a realm no sovran might of pain
Could crush, nor death with its ten thousand fears
Shock ; for thy brow that heaven's new glory wears
    Was helmed with honour and the high disdain
    For all things mean, and by thy life was plain
Love rules in right when love itself forswears.

Yet, gentle heart, though hands did never crown
    With gold of earth thy weary suffering head,
      At least one prince was in thy presence less,
One tyrant found his mastery overthrown—
    Death's darkness was as purple round thee shed,
      King, by true hope in utter hopelessness.

Albert Victor, Duke of Clarence.

JANUARY 14TH, 1892.

BLYTHE marriage bells already moved the air,
 The orange-blossom's scent was on the wind,
 Men said no hearts more royal or more kind
Would sway our England's sceptre, and would share
A nation's joy and sorrow.   Happy pair,
 Blest with the blessing of an equal mind,
 That Love had led a higher love to find,—
Love of the people and the people's care !

Then came another bride, whose icy breath
 Is only sweet for those who long to die,
  She came, she kissed our Prince and claimed
  his hand,
 And with one long exceeding bitter cry
  We cast the hopes and happiness we planned,
Heart-broken, at his feet—Bridegroom of Death !
D

The Crown of Tears.

ST. GEORGE'S CHAPEL, WINDSOR, JANUARY 20TH, 1892.

I HEARD the solemn ministry to pain
　　Those muffled drums and wailing trumpets made,
　　I saw the banners half-mast high displayed,
The slow sad-marching, melancholy train.
The steed, unmounted, went with sable rein
　　As if he knew the sorrow; cannonade
　　Came from the Royal slopes, and, overlaid
With flowers, we bore our young Prince home again.

I could not weep, there was so much in mind,
　　Dark town and towers and gorgeous chapel dim,
　　The mourning music and the silent bier;
But at the closing of that funeral hymn
One placed the crown a broken heart had twined
　　There on the coffin—and I felt the tear.

See Note 12.

HEROES AMONG MEN.

Sir John Franklin.

1786-1847.

(AT SPILSBY.)

WHEN from this street young Franklin watched
    the Bear

Turn in continual service to the Pole,

He must have marvelled with what strange control

That atom swayed the constellation near,

Some influence sure of that mysterious sphere

Touched then the mighty magnet of his soul,

To hold high purpose to its mighty goal,

And bid him for the cruel north-land steer.

Haply—for we who crawl upon this earth

Are moved by wings we wot not of at all—

From that far world a message at his birth

Grew as he grew, and framed his spirit's call,

And this poor town in humbleness has given

Proof that the patriot's heart is born in Heaven!

To the Memory of Lady Jane Franklin.

JULY 23RD, 1875.

QUIET and cold, and white as frozen snow !
   Well has the Master's cunning hand exprest
The honours on thine honourable breast,
The speaking eye, the calm command of brow—
Ah ! if those eyes could weep, they would weep now !
   To-day we carry to a well-earned rest
   One who hath need not any more of quest—
Whose love was champion of her marriage vow.

She needs no tomb, her monument shall be
The ancient bergs that build the Northern sea ;
   And when to summer waters melting slip
   Those giant crystals that enshrine thy ship,
The men that sail where thou and thine were found,
Shall tell the love no Arctic winter bound.

See Note 13.

Commander Wyatt Rawson.

SEPTEMBER 13TH, 1882.

BLAMELESS and lion-heart by land and sea,
  Oh ! wheresoever Christians seek their Lord
  And know Him in a life not idly poured,
But, at the desperate call that holds in fee
The bravest answer, poured unsparingly—
  The cost unrecked, the hazard hardly scored,—
  Obedience only waiting duty's word
To dare death's worst—who seek will meet with thee.

Whether they find thee with Amoaful's scars
  Fresh in the north's intolerable night,
    Lending thy comrades thine own body's fire,
Or, in close commune with Egyptian stars,
  The guide of moonless squadrons to the fight,
    Thyself to fall—thy fame to mount up higher.

See Note 14.

General Gordon.

JANUARY 26TH, 1885.

HERO of selfless heroes, resolute,
　　Simple in heart, of purpose crystal clear,
　　Ah! what availed that soul-perplexing year
Of lonely patience, expectation mute,
Those winks of watch dog slumber to recruit
　　Waste of long nights, and bid thee persevere
　　To build up ramparts in dark hearts of fear,
And pace the city wall with guardian foot!

Oh, what availed thy fruitless questioning
　　Of that beleaguered plain beyond the Nile,
　　　Whose dust-whirls never broke to flash of sword,
Volley of English cannon, and the ring
　　Of cheers from hearts that sought thee—this,
　　　　thine Isle,
　　　　Has learned how live and die, the warriors
　　　　of the Lord.

𝔉ather 𝔇amien.

APRIL, 1889.

NO golden dome shines over Damien's sleep;
A leper's grave upon a leprous strand
Where hope is dead, and hand must shrink from hand
Where cataracts wail towards a moaning deep,
And frowning purple cliffs in mercy keep
All wholesome life at distance, hath God planned
For him who led his saintly hero band,
And died a shepherd of Christ's exiled sheep.

O'er Damien's dust the broad skies bend for dome,
Stars burn for golden letters, and the sea
Shall roll perpetual anthem round his rest;
For Damien made the charnel-house life's home,
Matched love with death: and Damien's name
shall be
A glorious benediction world-possest.

At Livingstone's Funeral.

WESTMINSTER ABBEY, APRIL, 1874.

WHEN down the muffled melancholy nave
They bore the heart that ever yearned for home,
But ever felt its duty was to roam
Far wildernesses, solitary, brave,
That so who knew not home, sweet home might have—
Fierce nations to his funeral seemed to come,
To weep with those who underneath the dome
Wept for the friend they carried to his grave.

But we beheld upon that coffin borne
No wreaths of laurel, cypress or of bay,
Only the plumey feathers of the palm,
And as our voices rose in prayer and psalm
We saw one standing victor in the Morn,
And felt o'er darkened Africa the Day.

See Note 15.

LEADERS OF MEN.

At Hughenden.

19TH APRIL, 1881.

THE Primrose shines; unnoticed on the lawn

The Peacocks strut, they feel that it is spring,

They shake their fans, they drop their painted wing,

But Hughenden's white curtains all are drawn :

Who played the game of nations, King and Pawn,

Has played and lost the game where Death is King.

He nevermore shall see the cedars fling

Their fragrant shadows from the English dawn.

Ambitionless for self to be or have,

Ambitious for the land to be and do,

The Patriot-soul has vanished from our strife;

But, though his heart to dust and ashes go,

True Love shall bend above the threefold grave

That holds the friend, the statesman, and the wife.

𝕸. 𝕰. 𝕱orster.

F AREWELL, a sorrowing nation knows her need;
　　Farewell, farewell, the stormless time has come;
　　Farewell, we cannot grudge thee rest and home,
Nor with the strong pale angel will we plead,
Our leader back, a little while, to lead;
　　For now the seas of state are white with foam,
　　Perplexing winds of faction rave and roam;
Law-mongers creedless are; thou hadst a creed!

Firm patriot-will, fierce hater of misrule,
　　Fearlessly faithful when thy country called,
　　　　Thy soul was thy prime-minister, thy queen
　　　　Truth, with her simple law of "say and mean."
Stern breaker of the new tyrannic school,
　　Upholder of pure conscience, unenthralled.

John Bright.

MARCH 27TH, 1888.

L AST of the gladiators gone to rest !
   No more thy voice's trumpet-tone shall thrill
   The nations halting between good and ill;
Thy lion head has sunk upon thy breast,
But death has not annulled thy life's bequest—
   Unswerving right, inviolable will,
   To lead the sons of labour up the hill
Of Freedom, faithful, peaceful, soul-possessed.

Great Tribune of the people, storms may rise,
   They will not shake the pillars of thy throne,
      Seeing thy rule was selflessness sincere,
And praise did never blind those patient eyes
      That looked, beyond State discord, to the year
   When golden love shall bind all hearts in one.

Lord Carnarbon.

JUNE 28TH, 1890.

N OW let the Highclere cedars darklier wave
　　The rhododendrons fall and flush no more ;
　　A silent face beside the silent shore
Waits for the silent shrouding of the grave !
The patriot soul that dared alone be brave,
　　And from the hate of kings a false robe tore,
　　That bade all loyal hearts refill the store
Of England's love which shall our England save,

Moves crowned with lilies ; Learning sorrows near,
　　And golden speech that from the " Golden Grove "
　　Drew such sweet life, perforce must mutely bend.
But, ah, clear-souled Carnarvon, by thy bier
　　Two kneel, hands clasped triumphant; holy Love
　　And Faith that made the future firmest friend.

See Note 16.

𝔉𝔦𝔢𝔩𝔡 𝔐𝔞𝔯𝔰𝔥𝔞𝔩 𝔟𝔬𝔫 𝔐𝔬𝔩𝔱𝔨𝔢.

APRIL 24TH, 1891.

GREAT battle-thinker, war and work is o'er,
   No more shall hill and vale and blossoming plain
   Shine as a chequer-board whereon your brain
May plan for peace thro' victory, and no more
In thought shall cannon crown the heights and roar,
   Nor armies march and countermarch to gain
   The dread arbitrament of woe and pain,
Whereby men hold the fields they plowed of yore.

Your warfare is accomplished, you have gone
   To where men sheathe the sword and bear the palm,
   And Love leads on to fuller light and life ;
   Where souls, who through Earth's pettiness and
   strife
   Have held their strong simplicity and calm,
Hear, in the Land of Peace, Heaven's loud "Well done!"

E

SHEPHERDS OF MEN.

At Keble's Grave.

1792-1866.

At the head of the graves of Keble and his wife in Hursley Churchyard stands a cross; inscribed upon the base are the words :—"Quibus lux esto perpetua. Pax eterna."

O NE shadow only on their sleep can fall!

The long large-hearted glories of the west

That pierce the pines on Hursley's woody crest

And fire the steeple-vane, make rosy all

The cottage roofs, with splendour magical

Turn chalk to cliff of gold, and have possest

Yon glimmering weald with wonder, here may rest,

As long as bird to drowsy bird can call.

For here are lamps whose urns of faith and song

Nor grief nor death could shatter, now they shine

In worlds of peace that need not sun nor moon :

And rosy morn, red eve, or golden noon

Casts from one cross a shadow, that cross Thine,

Thou Lord of light for whom they waited long.

Charles Kingsley.

1819-75.

(OFF BIDEFORD BAY.)

BY wave-bruised Baggy Point, smooth Croyda's head,
  We crossed the bay of Danish Hubba's woe;
  High o'er the sea-grey beach of Westward Ho
The dunes on which thy sun its magic shed,
Gleamed doubly radiant; but our eyes were led
  To that white beacon-tower the sailors know,
  Star of the shoals where Taw and Torridge flow,
Friend for the lost, home-bringer from the dead.

For thou in perilous times of dark didst stand
  A beacon true no wanderer could reprove,
    Whether he tossed on doubt's unresting sea,
Or groped his way through reason's shifting sand,
    And many a soul steered straight for home by thee,
  Thou pure white tower of fire and faith and love.

Dean Stanley.

JULY 18TH, 1881.

THERE was a silence in the city's roar,
 And ere Saint Margaret's bell had ceased to boom,
 With sense of universal loss, the gloom
Saddened the land, and broke from shore to shore
In tides of lamentation :—Passed ! before
 True christian love could fill the teacher's room
 Or Time had fitted to her changing loom
The pattern of the charity he wore.

Fathered and tutored well, he never veiled
 For praise or gain the vision of his eye,
 Hard pressed, and dying with God's harness on.
But where keen sense and wit unblunted failed,
 His all-endearing personal presence won ;
 Now is he free, who fought for Liberty.

Dean Stanley.

BURIED IN WESTMINSTER ABBEY, JULY 27TH, 1881.

B URY the Dean where each familiar grave
    Opens in rival welcome for the guest
    Who quickened gloriously its dust, who best
In chapel dim, dark cloister's hoary nave,
Lit the gold lamps of history, and gave
    His nation's shrine a record to attest,
    That there in grateful honour lies at rest
The wise in truth, in deed the nobly brave.

Bury the Dean, and let no stinted praise
    Fall from the lips of men he soared above,
      Unfettered, striving still to reconcile
    Creeds past and present in the life of love,
      Else will the Dead he championed throng the aisle,
And the Great Ghosts loud acclamation raise.

The Stanley Monument in Rugby Chapel.

L IE here in quiet, let boy-gazers know
   How, even in sleep, the spirit of the man
   Moved, and the blood, though all was marble,
    ran
To fruitful issue thro' a heart of snow ;
Lie here above the world and close below
   Thy master. Let ambition plot and plan,
   Still shall the humble-hearted lead the van,
Their lives bequeathed to larger love shall grow.

Sleep on, thy rest no strife of tongues can break,
   But on thy face young eyes shall look and learn
   How they who seek pure wisdom never die,
   To this white form white souls shall ever fly ;
   Here from cold lips of stone new truths will burn,
And where thou sleepest Charity shall wake.

𝔐offat the 𝔐issionary.

AUGUST 8TH, 1883.

I HEARD that old Arch-Missionary say:—
"Grant me no Heaven to lose, no Hell to gain,
But give me youth, I every nerve would strain
To succour poor down-trodden Africa!"
Hero and priest, albeit thy locks are grey,
Thy hand, that fear and constant need did train,
That swayed a nation, clutched the lion's mane,
And strangled serpents, is as swift to-day?

We see thee ward the arrow, frame the plow,
Plead for God's Peace where chafing warriors sit,
Thine own tongue lost in exile, hardly thou
To our dull prose their poet-words dost fit!
While from the caves, beneath that tower of brow,
Flash the twin lamps Christ's quenchless love has lit!

See Note 17.

𝔓rincipal 𝔖hairp.

SEPTEMBER, 1885.

L ET Jura wail, the loud Atlantic sweep
To Argyle's inland solitudes forlorn,
By sound and firth let sobbing seas be borne
From that dark shore where song is laid asleep.
For never gentler heart did climb the steep
Unwavering, never holier oath was sworn
Than his, who in his youth's exalted morn
To nature gave his innocence to keep.

On ! lost from human presence, but unlost
To those who felt thy heart in thy right hand
And knew it beat in tune to all things good,
Sad are the vales of Wordsworth's Cumberland
And drear St. Andrews scholar-brotherhood,
But happier sure Heaven's love-enlightened host.

Bishop Fraser.

OCTOBER 22ND, 1885.

THE whole church prest her hand upon her heart
    With pain to hear thy heart had ceased to beat;
    There fell a shock of silence on the street,
And death a moment hushed the wrangling mart;
For thou wert of thy multitudes a part,
    Thy wisdom sat not only in the seat
    Of lore ecclesiastic, and thy feet
Were swift to heal the nation's every smart.

Oh! generous eyes, from purer heights to see
    The littleness of party—clearer now!
        Oh! voice not ever lifted but to serve
        The Christ of all the churches, and to nerve
Weak souls. Thy Shepherd-chief had need of thee,
    And lo His crown upon thy tireless brow

𝔅𝔦𝔰𝔥𝔬𝔭 𝔍𝔞𝔫𝔫𝔦𝔫𝔤𝔱𝔬𝔫.

MASSACRED WITH HIS FOLLOWERS IN MASAI LAND, CENTRAL
AFRICA, OCTOBER, 1885.

WHEN the assured and fore-determined day
 Shall flood the darker continent's dark heart,
 When warriors leave the spear for plow and mart,
And the white Christ assumes His gentle sway,
Then shall thy fifty followers where they lay
 In blood and silence, from their ashes start
 To bear thee witness, what august a part
Was thine—thou Shepherd-herald of the Way.

Those unresisting hands were fiercely bound,
 Thy soul was free, thy voice was loud in prayer
 Potent as Stephen's, e'er he fell asleep,
And if no Paul with hot assent was there,
Thy martyr summons went the wide world round,
 The crimson seed is sown, the Church shall reap.

Principal Tulloch.

1886.

GONE to the land of light and calm in fear
  For this dark day and our tempestuous time,
  Already hast thou heard the silver chime,
That ever doth our jarring earth ensphere.
Nor art thou friendless, thy devout compeer[1]
  Who shared the toil of thy laborious prime
  Comes from those rosy mountains angels climb:—
Friendship on earth, in Heaven is love more dear.

And if before thine ears were stopped by death
  No message came of that last battle cry,
    Where men fought fierce with argument for swords
Thou knowest now, from out our cloudy breath
    And strife of indistinguishable words,
  God rolls his car of Truth to Victory.

See Note 18.

[1] Principal Shairp.

Edward Thring.

HEADMASTER OF UPPINGHAM.

1853-1887.

LORD of the Lion-heart, with soul of thought,
    In no vain mould of mere expedient cast,
  He dared to stand against the public blast
Of opposition, for the truths he taught.
In fire from pagan page and Scripture caught
    He forged the present to a helpful past;
    Whate'er of life he learned, he held it fast,
And wove it into beauty as he wrought.

Preacher and poet, with the prophet eyes
    To see in boys the men our time should need,
      He found, for dullest clay, some grace God-given,
    On quickened furrows flung his living seed,
Set Learning in her fair fit Paradise,
      And showed how Love, not Knowledge led to
      Heaven.

Edward Thring.

OCTOBER 22ND, 1887.

L OVED Father of the schoolboy multitude,
  Friend of their short swift ages passed away
  Guide of their labour, champion of their play,
Who dared for zeal of noble masterhood
To stand alone, a rock above the flood
  Of easy acquiescence, and gainsay
  The dazzling bright ambitions of to-day
That tempt to learning's heights the scholar brood,

Thy presence fails for solace or command,
  Thy soul is ours, thou great schoolmaster-king;
  Still, father of thy children fatherless,
  Unto thy voice of cheer the pupils press,
And hearts that honour truth in every land,
  Can hear thy voice for truth and honour ring.

Bishop Lightfoot.

DECEMBER 21ST, 1889.

IN the Prince Bishop line, the princeliest thou
  Being the humblest soul, since Leader's son
  Saw angel hosts ascending, and was won
To leave his fold and take the preacher's vow.
From Farne to Camus' flood in grief we bow,
  Northumbria's flock is smitten and alone,
  For thou, the Shepherd, to far fields art gone.
Life claimed thee consecrate. Death sealed thy brow.

Chief lord, among thy scholars scholar still !
  Thou guider of earth's flock, thyself heaven-guided,
    By what calm waters, and what pastures sweet
Dost thou in glory minister, whose will
    Was to make strong and whole a church divided
      And bring the bruised and out-cast to Christ's
      feet ?

F

Dean Oakley.[1]

JUNE 10TH, 1890.

H ERE am I wrapped about with sun and showers
  Among the hills that often gave you call,
    Blue hills that gleamed so near to Carlisle's wall,
That seemed so far from dark Mancunium's towers;
And you are wrapped about with cloud of flowers,
  Or lie beneath the purple sunless pall,
    In some sad Cymric village, and tears fall,
And bells are muffled, for the Lord of mowers
Has, in His June-tide mowing, touched your field:
  But God doth know that never heart did beat
  For poor man's wants and woes with surer heat,
    And they who follow on Christ's sheaves to bind
    In fallows where you sowed, shall surely find
Life's joy hath increase, Love—a larger yield.

[1] Dean first of Carlisle, and afterwards of Manchester.

Archbishop Thomson.

CHRISTMAS DAY, 1890.

D EAD, did you say? York's good Archbishop dead!—
Brimful of human knowledge, and so wise
In that diviner world's simplicities—
Then breaks a pillar, falls a church's head,
Who dared, alone, the shepherd heights to tread,
And in a day of mist and various cries
Taught work for others was man's sacrifice,
And held that truth, unswerving, Heavenward led.

And as, when first round shepherds there was poured
The light of Christmas, while the angels sang,
They rose with joy and left their smouldering fires;
So, when our bells the Christmas message rang,
When rocked the clamorous towers, and shook the
spires,
He left the crook, and went to greet his Lord.

Cardinal Newman.

1801-90.

HE lies in state, whose soul was far above
    The earthly dress that we men Honour call;
    He rests and speaks not underneath the pall,
Whose voice was loud for duty and for love.
He walks in state, whose spirit mates above
    With spirits never held by flesh in thrall;
    He speaks with angels, No more Cardinal,
Servant of truths he sought on earth to prove.

And knowing all the followers of One Light,
    And known by One, of all the Churches Lord,
      He finds Heaven's way the way of children still,
The way of little ones, who seeing right,
    Do it, and ask not of hard Reason's word,
      And seek the Father by the Father's will.

Canon Liddon.

BURIED AT ST. PAUL'S, SEPTEMBER 16TH, 1890.

IN olden time, the prophet of the Lord
   Went up on glorious chariot-wheels of flame,
   But this pure heart, returning whence it came,
Had need of no fire-horses, for his word
Clothed him with light, and his keen spirit's sword
   Flashed lightning as he spoke of Christ's dear name,
   And in his splendid carelessness of fame
He shone transfigured, till, the silver cord
Loosed here, he soared to Heaven. Though nevermore
   Above the whispers of that mighty dome
     His golden voice shall echo in the soul,
     There is, within Death's sudden thunder-roll,
The whisper of a glory gone before—
   A prophet-cry to call us nearer home.

Archbishop Magee.

TRANSLATED FROM PETERBORO'. DIED MAY 4TH, 1891.

H E scarce had known the walls of great De Gray,
　　Had hardly seen, where silent Ouse doth flow,
　　How tutelary elms and poplars grow
About the palace garden—when the day
Predestined came to call his soul away,
　　And underneath that triple-caverned row
　　Of pillared portals, solemnly and slow
We bore his bones to mingle with the clay
Of Aelfric, and of Kinsius: but his voice,
　　His wholesome wit, his reasonable mind,
　　　These were not coffined with him, these remain:
　　　And Yorkshire's Viking, Peterboro's Dane,
　　Still feel the gift which came upon the wind
That sealed with tongues of flame the Spirit's choice.

See Note 19.

Bishop Goodwin.

NOVEMBER 25TH, 1892.

HERE in the land of shepherds let him rest—
Chief shepherd he of Cumbria's ancient wild—
And lay his bones beside his well-loved child,
And strew the snow-white flowers upon his breast;
For he with childhood's joyousness was blest,
   With manhood's calm; to any weakling mild,
   Fierce only to the wolves; and unbeguiled
By soft vale voices sought the mountain crest,
And on the peaks of duty, not of fame,
   Wrought out his shepherd's calling. Now he lies
   In sight of Skiddaw, and the hearts that burn—
Remembering all the deeds of Kentigern—
Know, since, till this man taught us, none more wise
To lift the cross, beside the Derwent came.

At Bishop Goodwin's Grave.

THE DAY AFTER THE FUNERAL. NOVEMBER 29TH, 1892.

HERE rests from earthly labour, not from love,
  A strenuous heart, strong hand and tireless brain,
  One who thro' death's dark gate unhurt of. pain
And quite unquenched of spirit, went to prove
The glory of full being: oh, remove
  This weary weight of death that doth restrain
  The ardour of his going! grant again
Sight of the Shepherd passed to fields above!

Nay, since, dear God and Father of us all,
  Thou at Thy time dost give Thy loved ones sleep,
    We would not ask our Shepherd from the
      height,
    Nor claim him back to darkness from the light;
  Only we pray Thee, with a clearer call
Call close around the cross Thy sorrowing sheep.

Cardinal Manning.

ON HEARING OF HIS LAST ILLNESS, JANUARY, 1892.

$\mathbf{M}$AY God's sweet sun of health shine out and move
The bitter cloud that darkens on our hopes,
For you thro' strength and weakness up the slopes
Of Faith have passed unfaltering : Heaven above
Smiles on you; not for ring or jewelled glove,
Wrappings of scarlet, gorgeous golden copes,
Not for the kissing of the hand of popes,
But for your kiss of peace, your cloak of love.

Frail were your hands and frail your voice's call—
Both strong for right; Faith helped your high
endeavour
When wealth and work stood angrily at strife.
Ah! though your feet are near that other river,
Stay with us still, for England needs your life,
Friend of the poor! wise-counselling Cardinal!

At the Lying in State of Cardinal Manning.

JANUARY 19TH, 1892.

H E lies in purple, as becomes a man
　　Of royal nature, round him starry bright
　　Stand the dark walls in token of our night.
Those aged feet that still so swiftly ran
To succour, those grey eyes that seemed to scan
　　The worlds unseen, have lost their power and light,
　　And the frail hands, and strenuous for the right,
Are cold.　Mourns England, grieves the Vatican !

Yet death has set his forehead free from lines,
　　The golden crook is idle at his side,
　　He lies at rest and on his purple glove
Like flame unwaveringly the topaz shines,
　　While o'er him dead there bends the One who died,
　　With arms outstretched—the image of his love.

Spurgeon.

FEBRUARY 4TH, 1892.

Neither for rugged wit nor Saxon phrase,
  Oh mourners by the soft Italian sea—
Blue as the sapphire lake of Galilee
Whereby in thought he laboured all his days—
This prophet last of Puritans—we praise,
  But rather that he never bowed the knee
  To false expedient, ever flung out free
The banner of a gospel he upraised.

Not on the hills with peace his feet were shod,
  No desert silence by his voice surprised
    Heard the clear note "Repent ye of your sin";
    But in the midst of mammon's busiest din
He dared, each day rededicate to God,
  To cry aloud "Believe and be baptised."

Bishop Phillips Brooks.

DIED AT BOSTON, 23RD JANUARY, 1893.

YOU came, and with you came a wind from Heaven
  The health and vigour of Atlantic gales,
  Our hearts revived, our souls reset their sails,
And with new courage o'er dark seas were driven.
Weak knees were strong which hopelessly had striven,
  Tired hands that felt—what agony avails !
  Cast overboard all this world's cumbrous bales,
Took in fresh hope and life your lips had given.

There as we heard the passionate appeal,
  And watched your body swayed beneath the stress
  Of half you felt, of all you could express,
    We learned again how sped the Holy Ghost
    Thro' flame and wind of that first Pentecost,
And knew your message by the Saviour's seal.

SINGERS AMONG MEN.

𝔇antt 𝔊abriel 𝔕ossetti.

APRIL 9TH, 1882.

G ONE down to take Proserpina the flowers,
Those daffodils let fall from Pluto's wain!
The grey old bard, who bound with silver chain
Of simple song his western home to ours,
Waits, happy for thy guidance to the bowers
Where, guests long since in thy mysterious train,
The singers sit right glad to entertain
Thee with thy later tale of Tuscan towers.

Thou Painter-Poet, with the brow divine,
Whereon was set some memory of his face
Who gave our England song for evermore,
Thy 'House of Life' is broken, but back to shore
Comes Charon, with that sonnet-toll of thine
Which Death dared never keep in his dark place.

See Note 20.

Jenny Lind.

NOVEMBER 2ND, 1887.

NEVER again to see an English Spring!
  Never to watch the purple copses burn,
  The gold gay-hearted daffodil return!
Never to hear the lark above me sing
And climbing up his stair ring after ring,
  Send consolation earthwards! how I yearn
  But once, once more, to find the bracken fern
Lifting to fragrant light its fairy wing!

The Malvern valleys, mist-enshrouded, wait,
  The Malvern hills are shuddering into snow,
    But thou clear-throated angel-heart of Dawn,
Thou standest now within the happier gate
  Whence all the springs with life and love shall flow,
    To thrill the nightingale and flush the lawn.

See Note 21.

𝔐𝔞𝔱𝔱𝔥𝔢𝔴 𝔄𝔯𝔫𝔬𝔩𝔡.

IN LALEHAM CHURCHYARD, APRIL, 1888.

GONE, without word, or touch, or hint of pain
 Where the great visions of his earthly chase—
Sweet light and truth, and soul-appealing grace—
Stand full embodied. Surely not in vain
Our generation felt his high disdain
 For all that narrowed good to time and race;
 For all that wept in sordid common-place,
Or held life cramped in fashion's thoughtless chain.

Child of the Thames and Rotha,[1] o'er his rest
 The poplar grieves, the river sobs and cries,
 And souls that still unsatisfied must long
To know the highest and to think the best,
 Sigh, in accord, the human undersong
 Of loss, about the grave where Arnold lies.

[1] These are the rivers that seem specially associated with
Matthew Arnold's life and song,

Horatius Bonar.

31ST JULY, 1889.

SINGER, at length thy travelling days are done,
  And thou who heard'st the voice of Jesus say,
"Come unto me and rest," hast ceased thy lay,
Into the land of silence thou hast gone !
But still thy pure harp's high and holy tone—
  Harp strung in stern old covenanter's day—
  Sounds out, to cheer the pilgrim on his way
With echoes of the song about the Throne.

Still wheresoe'er the children's hymn may rise,
  Or the great congregation's voice upswell
    In plenitude of praise, thy clear heart's chord
Shall vibrate, till we hear in Paradise
    How all on earth, in sea, and Heaven that dwell,
      With one loud Alleluia bless the Lord.

Robert Browning.

DECEMBER 12TH, 1889.

BROWNING is dead at Venice! dark and slow
   The gondoliers move silently along,
  Wan Adria's sea sobs sorrowful among
Drear halls, and pale for grief sits Asolo.
Browning is dead! the voice tolls to and fro
   And hushes all his latest tender song,
   As in an organ when the deep notes throng
To drown the quavering treble's passionate flow.

Browning is dead! with Florence on his heart
   Writ large; but larger, England underneath—
    The England of his helping; for he knew
  The mind where Freedom is, and, to the death,
For souls in pain who dare the Angel part,
   Onset and victory his brave trumpet blew.

Robert Browning.

WESTMINSTER ABBEY, DECEMBER 30TH, 1889.

FROM Rivo Alto's silent palace hall,

From San Michele's wilderness of flowers,

Comes one for rest beneath our Abbey Towers

Whose song and soul shall never sleep at all.

The crown of Venice shines above the pall,

A brighter crown thy tireless spirit dowers,

For thy strong heart the weakest heart empowers

To "strive and thrive," fare forward, though we fall.

Singer of resolute right, and souls on fire

To meet the morrow's battle, and the 'must'

Of Truth triumphant with our latest breath,

Lie here, for gentle Spenser can desire

No knightlier guest, nor Chaucer in his dust

A truer harp. Lie here—here comes no death.

A Cry from Florence.

DECEMBER 12TH, 1889.

TAKE home the heart, her heart that cannot rest
　　Though in Etruria's southern-natured ground,
　　Take home the heart that fire and fulness found
In that sure heart whose secret she possest,
Take home the heart, the heart that at its best
　　Was bettered for his singing, whose strong sound
　　Was sweeter by her song, for she was crowned
Queen of a heart that was her King confest.

Hearts such as these have never ceased from beating,
　　Hearts such as these by sympathy divine
　　　Will palpitate in death, harmonious measure.
And still I hear a spirit voice entreating,
　　Let Arno give the Thames her poet-treasure,
　　One grave the dust of two immortals' shrine.

See Note 22.

James Russell Lowell.

AUGUST 12TH, 1891.

LOWELL is dead! a gold link snapt and gone
 That bound the Mother to the Daughter-land.
 Lowell is dead! I hear upon the strand
The mourning of two nations joined as one
Mixed with the drear Atlantic's monotone.
 For who will touch the harp with lighter hand,
 And who in time of tyrannous hate shall stand
And sing back Truth and Freedom to their throne?

Oh ! Stars that after dimness bless the night,
 Stripes rent, and with a people's heart-blood healed,
  Blow still mast-high, your poet speaks no more.
  But though this stroke of death has wounded sore
 The common heart to which his heart appealed,
Above our heads his star of Love is bright.

Lowell's Last Dream.

BEFORE he entered to Heaven's imperial Hall
    Where Light and Love and Beauty only reign,
    Unto his dying eyes a vision plain
Of kingly people met for festival
Came with triumphant pomp, and clarion call;
    And rising up with will to entertain
    Those goodly visitants, the courtier's brain
Reeled, and to death's dark arms did Lowell fall.

Not without presage of a royal home,
    Where, King of kings and Lord of lords, our God
      Crowns the true soul that nobly strives and sings
Of Right and Freedom, did that pageant come;
    With sovereign powers he long had made abode,
      For men who have the poet's heart are kings.

See Note 23.

The Centenary of Mozart.

DECEMBER 4TH, 1891.

G OD called whom for too short a time he gave,
　　Dust back to dust, snapped string and broke
　　the shell,
　And as they bore him towards the tolling bell
Of old St. Marx, no hands were there to wave
Adieu, no mourners but the winds that rave,
　　The tears shed for him were the rains that fell,
　　But all the hearts that ever felt his spell
Stand bowed to-day beside that pauper grave.

Mozart, thy soul, familiar grown with Death
　　Long since, laid willing touch upon the door
　　　That opened to the land where sorrows cease,
　　And leaving here on earth th' unfinished score
Went onward, singing, with an angel's breath,
　　　The requiem music of eternal peace.

𝔚alt 𝔚hitman.

MARCH 26TH, 1892.

DEAD is the "tan-faced" poet of the west,
   Blunt-mouthed, bluff-headed, he who dared to
   say
That for new freedom's democratic day
Thought should be free.   By no rhyme-fetters prest,
He bade his rude unmetred verse attest
   That drum-tap music suited well the way
   Of those who marched, head up, for labour's fray,
And rugged truth in nakedness was best.

Dead, but not dead the hope for which he toiled,
   Hope for the time when heart will speak to heart
      With its own rhythmic utterance, making men
Singers indeed ; and hands by labour soiled
      May feel each day they hold the poet's pen—
. And the shy seer shall no more dwell apart.

John Greenleaf Whittier.

SEPTEMBER 7TH, 1892.

WE shall not see again the deep-set eyes,
  Tight mouth, thought-furrows on the friendly face
  That never disavowed the Quaker race.
His shock of years is garnered under skies
Well known, well sung of, for his soul was wise
  With all the change of season, and the grace
  Of Nature, stored afield in lonely place,
To melt the labourer's heart with melodies.

His voice was clear because he saw the truth,
  The simple truth that God would have men free,
    On furrows red with war his seed was sown;
    And loving right and hating tyranny,
  He fashioned for a nation in its youth
    Such music as its age shall not disown.

See Note 24.

THINKERS AMONG MEN.

Carlyle.

CHELSEA, FEBRUARY 5TH, 1881.

THRO' mist and gloom, indignant and alone,
   He nursed his heart's great fire, he spake his lore ;
   Death smoothed at last the lines that sorrow wore,
And nations mourned a master spirit gone.
Of all our prophet saviours, last but one,
   Breaker of idols, stern-voiced counsellor,
   Shall England hear thy Doric phrase no more,
Hear and obey the village craftsman's son.

Nay, long as Thames shall roll toward the Town
   Its gathered freshness from a thousand vales
      To pass in sorrow on towards the sea,
His words of truth shall sound tho' tyrants frown,
   His courage keep us when our courage fails,
      His sadness to our gladness strength shall be.

Thomas Hill Green.

OXFORD, MARCH 26TH, 1882.

H USHED be the bells of all his city towers,
    We need no sound to swell the deep "alas!"
    Let Isis move unsobbing thro' the grass,
The sun shine still upon the Nuneham flowers.
He was of those rare hearts whom nature dowers
    With unassuming quietude, his glass
    Turned all reflection inwards, men might pass
Nor know the depth and splendour of his powers.

Hew him of granite, granite was his mind,
    Give him the sword, for trenchant was his thrust,
    And cast these purblind late philosophies
Prone at his feet who trod them into dust.
Then write him, " Patriot that no bribes could blind,
    Prophet of Truth, sure Teacher of the Wise."

Dr. John Brown.

DIED AT EDINBURGH, MAY 11TH, 1882.

LANARK, the sun upon thy moors had power
　To sow a human heart with golden seed.
And heard in distance, tenderly, the Tweed
Nursed with its dews an everlasting flower
Of such exceeding radiance, such a dower
　Of genial blessing, such a heavenly breed,
　That where it bloomed all other seemed but weed,
And barren waste became an angel's bower.

Nor vainly did the pastor's large-eyed child
　Race with the collie, learn the shepherd's stride,
　And bear the yeanling in his plaid : who, grown,
　Gave audience to each creature's voice that cried,
　Carried his brother's burdens with his own
And left the sick ones whole because he smiled.

John Richard Green.

1837-1883.

The inscription upon the marble slab in the cemetery of Mentone concludes with the words :—" He died learning."

SO die we all, the sun o'er Agal's height
   That sinks unto its setting could not know
   How this high terraced rock of rest would glow
With glory unimagined, how its light
Would pierce the cypress shadow, and make bright
   As molten gold these pillars white as snow
   That guard the marble whose dark letters show,
Here lies the learner who could read aright

The story of our England. Souls like thine,
   Truth seeker ! glad to learn as glad to teach,
     So keen in quest for knowledge, so sincere,
     These having learned earth's simple letters here,
See at life's sunset nobler light can shine,
   Find Heaven's full wisdom, speak with angel speech.

Dr. Döllinger.

JANUARY 10TH, 1890.

PURE-HEARTED servant of the Living God,
  Sure scholar, trained by Truth's unswerving hand,
  High leader of high Love's triumphant band,—
Christ you obeyed but not his "Vicar's" nod:
Silent you kissed the inevitable rod,
  Owned no soul-quenching hierarch's demand,
  And passed for Faith, Faith's exile thro' the land,
Nor chose the easier way unreason trod.

Clouds came between, and death, with cloudier bar,
  Has come, but round your sovran Sun, in light,
  Turns the true soul that set so many free:
  Still as for dawn above a troublous sea
To you men yearn: yea, in her darkest night
The church that scorned shall hail your guiding star!

H

Lord Justice General Englis.

AUGUST 20TH, 1891.

THE corn was yellow by the Lowland braes,
 The Highland heather purple on the hill,
When he our nation honoured for his skill,
And store of mellow wisdom, whom we praise
For justice and for judgment—strong to raise
 A standard to reflect the Almighty's will,
 Bowed his grey head, and fearing nothing ill
Bore to God's Hall of Judgment all his days
Of fulness and endeavour. Lead him in,
 Ye powers of gentle innocence! Give place,
  Ye angels sworn to righteousness! His mind
Cared for the moulding of a righteous race;
He judged men's deeds, to Heaven he left the sin,
 And blessed with wise benevolence his kind.

Sir George Airy, K.C.B.

DIED JANUARY 2ND, 1892, IN HIS 91ST YEAR.

FOR full three generations had he known
    Sunlight and starlight, then at last there came
    An angel with a chariot of flame,
And he went forth thro' stellar spaces sown
Thick with the seed of suns, beyond the cone
    Of planetary systems none might name,
    Till new light dazed him, and he heard acclaim
Of praise around the great Creator's throne.

He stood and bowed his head before the light
    Those only see whose hearts are pure and blest
    With child-like love and reverence, then he cried—
" Though never more can come the purple night
    With wondrous gleam of worlds, here let me rest.
    Thee, Lord, I sought, my soul is satisfied."

John Couch Adams.

THE ENGLISH DISCOVERER OF THE PLANET NEPTUNE.
DIED AT CAMBRIDGE, JANUARY 21ST, 1892.

GOD stretched His jewelled splendour far and wide

    Above the Cornish moorlands, there He met

A boy, and from dark fallows dewy-wet

Bade him look up. He, scholar grown, espied

The wandering of lone Uranus, and plied

    Star-quest in heights abysmal, till his net

    Of calculations intricate had set

Sure, but unseen, far Neptune at the side

Of that perturbéd planet. Then was hurled

    Space from its throne, and distance was enchained,

      And mind flung back the gates of ultimate gloom—

But little said the seeker, he who gained

      Glory for England in his narrow room,

Wherein he searched the Heavens and found a world.

R. L. Nettleship.

DIED ON MOUNT BLANC, AUGUST 25TH, 1892.

WHEN God from off life's perilous slope doth call
   His men of humble heart to go up higher,
   He sends for this the chariot wheels of fire,
For that the torrent thundering to the fall,
Snow-avalanche, ice-plumed wings of storm; and all
   Who hear the dreadful courier coming nigher
   Sink into silence, leave their last desire
Dumb before One who holdeth speech in thrall.

But this brave soul of pure unselfishness
   Sang till the dawn to cheer his comrade band,
   Then marched right on to death upon the height,
And, since in alien tongue he needs must bless,
   Reached dying hands with longing infinite
   Which spake farewells that all might understand.

See Note 25.

Renan.

OBIIT, PARIS, OCTOBER 2ND, 1892.

R ENAN is gone, we shall not see him more,
    That massive face, those eyes of twinkling grey,
    The prince of cynics—he has passed away
Who rich in wisdom made his brothers poor :
He, entering the inevitable door,
    Has heard the truth that never can betray
    Crying :—" Behold your puppets at a play
Are living souls upon no phantom shore."

For now at length is variance reconciled
    Between the reason and the faith of man,
      The double soul that so perplexed his life
      Has ceased from irremediable strife,
    The Christ he dwarfed fills out to godlike span,
The God he doubted claims again his child.

Sir Richard Owen.[1]

DECEMBER 18TH, 1892.

H E saw the light on Morecambe's golden sands,
The crooked Lune ran silver to the main,
And he went seawards, but his soul was fain
By helm of thought to seek for other lands
And sound the deep of knowledge. To his hands
Earth gave primeval secrets, o'er the plain
Flew bat-winged pterodactyls, once again
Through swamp and ooze the Saurian pushed in bands.

Revealer of the times of tooth and claw,
He filled the world with dragons ; bone by bone
Guessed at the bird Dinornis great and grim,
But as he listened to the blackbird's hymn
He heard a prophet voice, an angel tone
Sing of a higher life with Love for Law.

---

[1] Owen was born at Lancaster, and as a lad went to sea.

FRIENDS AND NEIGHBOURS.

E. P. Seeley.

DIED IN THE LEBANON, ENGAGED IN MISSION WORK,
OCTOBER 25TH, 1881.

HIGH on the hills we laid her in repose,
　　And left our treasure, but we little wist
　How soon the ranges of deep amethyst
That roll up heavenward to the Syrian snows
Would yield to this one jewel where it glows
　　Midway 'twixt blue and blue.　Beloved of Christ,
　　Not vainly was thy pure life sacrificed
For Him who led thee bravely to the close.

Where'er among the vales of Lebanon
　　Between the olives and the mulberries
　　　We catch a glimpse of Him they crucified,
　　We see thee ever walking at His side,
　　And by the fuller sunlight of thine eyes
We know thy heart its happiness has won.

The Painter's Home-Going.

IN MEMORIAM G. Q. P. TALBOT,
OBIIT MAY 28TH, 1885.

GOD calls us when our eyes can bear the sight
Of all his lovelinesses—lest our mind
Should by the sudden beauty be smit blind—
To that new land, where neither sun gives light
Nor moon, but glowing love hath banished night
And sorrow with the night. 'Look not behind,
But go: thine eyes are ready—thou shalt find
Power to behold, with joyance infinite.'

Thereon, without a sigh the painter rose,
Yea, with a smile he laid his palette by;
Long had he looked beyond the sunset bars,
Had felt a pureness whiter than the snows,
Had heard the immortal music of the stars,
And knew that love for beauty could not die.

Auguste Guyard.

BARMOUTH.

HERE lies a man who toiled with pen and spade,
  Who went forth sowing, and with all his might
  Wrought, from the dawn, until the sunset light—
And so from barren Rock an Eden made—
Who, sworn all truth and all things pure to aid,
  Of all things beautiful the Gentle Knight,
  Still faced the storm, still battled with the blight,
And plied unmurmuringly his Heavenly trade.

To this high crag, beloved of him, he gave
  His out-worn body, trusting so the weed
    Of some wild saxifrage would kindlier grow
    Above his ashes laid in peace below.
He little thought that from his hermit grave
  Would bloom, for aye, Love's universal seed.

A Peaceful End.

CROSS SYKE, 1886.

GOD calls His well-beloved in various wise,
    Now with a shock that rends the Temple wall
  So swift, the soul before the tower can fall
Flies scared above the ruin : now, her eyes
Almost familiar grown with Paradise,
    The faithful watcher hears the angel call ;
    While some scarce seem to wait for death at all,
Just fall asleep and wake with Heaven's surprise.

And such wert thou—so gently didst thou pass
    But that thine eyes irrevocably set
      On that transfiguring glory, could not look
Our way, we had not guessed thy pure life's glass
    Was run, but rather deemed thee with us yet,
      Thy face to smile a moment from thy book.

𝔈. 𝔅. and 𝔉. 𝔖. 𝔖. 𝔅.

DROWNED WHILST SAILING ON DERWENTWATER IN A SQUALL,
SEPTEMBER 9TH, 1886.

FROM the dark deeps of this our endless woe,
To those dark deeps that stopped such manly breath,
Like one in fear, who, halting, listeneth
If any call, our hearts flit to and fro,
Your voices sound not, but one voice I know—
It is the solemn sovereign voice of Death :
" There is a world beyond this world," it saith,
" There is a deep to which thou canst but go."

Untimely lost ! and only back to come
With speechless mouth, calm faces, sightless eyes,
Well have ye ridden out Earth's wildest gale,
Companions still with Christ aboard ye sail,
A ship of life, whose port is Paradise,
And freighted full of love ye steer for Home.

John Richardson.

CUMBERLAND POET AND SCHOOLMASTER, ST. JOHN'S VALE.
APRIL 30TH, 1886.

O NEVER clad in academic gown,
   To wisdom led the simpler cottage way;
   By nature tended till thy head was grey,—
The heart of nature grew into thine own;
And whether 'neath Helvellyn's moorland brown,
   Along by glittering Bure thy steps would stray,
   A poet-angler's, or, on market-day,
Among the yeomen of our village town,

Above thy estate thy soul did ever soar,
   Beyond thy mortal sight thine eyes could see
      And the poor scholars at their upland school
      Learned of thee this—the Poet's golden rule—
   That eyes and hearts were given to man to be
On earth the gatherers of a heavenly lore.

Life-boat Heroes.

THE UPSETTING OF THE ST. ANNE'S LIFEBOAT.
DECEMBER, 1886.

L OST in the passionate surges of the sea,
   Lost in the moonwhite waters and the wind,
   Our hearts that follow after them, shall find
Their souls unhurt where'er their bodies be.
For they have out-faced Death, and they are free,
   Free with the name of Heroes, and the mind
   Of Him who died to succour human kind,
For life they gave their own a willing fee.

Their babes may wail, their wives and lovers weep,
   Sad tides may drift their treacherous boat ashore
      And moan along the melancholy sands;
      But when the rocket leaps with faithful hands
   I know strong hearts will pull as stout an oar
And breast a fiercer storm for those who sleep.

I

Life through Death.

THE COLLIERY EXPLOSION AT ST. HELENS, WORKINGTON.
APRIL 19TH, 1888.

D EEP in the earth's dark womb that teemed with
    death,
  From morn till eve the brave men laboured on,
  No stay nor rest the desperate task had won,
But still they fought the fierce cave's fiery breath;
Came forth a spell at sundown, saw the heath
  And vale and sea burn glorious, then cried one:
  "Better to bide above, our work half-done,
Than back return to fight and fail beneath."

"Nay," answered others, "hark, our bairns and wives
  Call to us, 'Save the pit and save our bread!'
  Half work is no work for our hands to do."
And down they went, the quick to join the dead,
  The flame-blast broke, and God's clear voice
    rang thro'—
"Who labour thus and lose shall save their lives."

Ned Brown.

KILLED AT HIS POST, THORNTHWAITE MINES, 1889.

YOU knew Ned Brown, no kinder truer hand
  E'er plied the pick, and found beneath the earth
Laborious bread. Our Father knew his worth:
He keeps New Year in Heaven, our Fatherland;
No more beneath the stars at work's command,
  His steps shall ring, his cheery voice make mirth,
  Nor shall he, home returned at morning's birth,
For some friend's sake forego the sleep he planned.

But still between the Derwent and the hills
  That rise against our golden gleaming west
    His honest tread shall sound upon the road,
    And they who sink the shaft, and seek the lode,
  Shall hear Ned's voice come sounding 'mid the drills,
  "Fall at your work, boys: falling so is best."

The Poet's 'Lilian.'

IN MEMORY OF S. E. SHAWELL.
OCTOBER 14TH, 1889.

COME to the grave, and tell her we have met,
   Bid her come forth, and smile once more, once
      more;
   But ah ! the deep earth and the fast-closed door
And the green grass with tears, not dewdrops, wet !
Dear soul, whose laughing eyes were ever set
   To fill the dark with light, to make with store
   Of simple kindness for the rich and poor
A crown of joy, thou hast thy coronet.

And we, who stand and sorrow without words
   Because one more of those, who through life's span
      Brightened the earth, has passed beyond recall,
We say, "She once was ours, she is the Lord's,
   She whom the poet sang of, 'Lilian,'
      Sings now in Heaven and smiles upon us all."

𝔐𝔞𝔯𝔶 𝔖𝔱𝔞𝔫𝔤𝔢𝔯.

FIELDSIDE, KESWICK, FEBRUARY 5TH, 1890.

CHILD of the brother to that generous man
   Who, vowed to Death, bequeathed his friend
   release
From trivial care, and gave the Muses ease,
And set laborious Wordsworth in the van—
You knew 'Nurse Wilsey,' coaxed old 'Clogger Dan,'
   Climbed unreproved on Southey's genial knees,
   Watched for the bard's homecoming through the trees,
And, wreath in hand, to crown the Laureate ran.

Bright shone the sun, the Crosthwaite bells rang clear,
   When blue-eyed Sara and that Rydal maid,
   The gentle Dora, tended you as bride.
But now another bridal morn is here,
   Christ in the heavens has called you to His side,
   And all the vale is rolled from sun to shade.

See Note 26.

Last of the Dorothys that Rydal knew.

GREEN-BANK, AMBLESIDE.

LAST of the Dorothys that Rydal knew
 In those drear days of old, when gathered round
 The morning table, Catherine was not found,
Nor Thomas, sleeping both beneath the dew,
Thy face was then so radiant, grief withdrew,
 Joy came, the children played on Rydal Mound,
 New hope sprang up like flowers from out the
 ground,
Birds sang again and life and laughter grew.

Not thine to lend the poet heart and will,
 Not thine to be a soft perpetual voice
 To keep the father's soul for ever young
 And e'en in death to speak a daughter's tongue.
 Rather in poor men's memories thine the choice
To make the name of Wordsworth fragrant still.

See Note 27.

Good-bye, Old Friend, Good-bye!

THE FUNERAL, FEBRUARY 25TH, 1890.

L IGHT on the land, but darkness with it dwells,
   Though gladlier never blushed the birch hard by
   Nor Bratha's alders to a bluer sky
In rosier fulness shone; for muffled bells
Ring up the Vale their sorrowful farewells,
   And with a human heart they seem to cry,
   While those six words, "Good-bye, old friend,
   good-bye,"
Float forth and sob to silence on the fells,

Good-bye, old friend, good-bye! the people move
   Like a dark flood toward the churchyard ground,
   The hymn is sung, the wreath is left to fade;
But ninety years of graciousness and love
   Were never yet within earth's bosom laid,
   Thou still art here, for all the sad bells sound.

See Note 27.

James Lappin.

LATE CHAIRMAN OF THE LIVERPOOL STOCK EXCHANGE.
OCTOBER 25TH, 1890.

HERE let white-handed Commerce weep and bend
 With purest-hearted Honour o'er the bier;
 A Prince of all integrity lies here;
Who from the dawn to the swift daylight's end,
Himself for others willingly would spend;
 Who walked with Justice, sworn to persevere,
 With Love and Reverence holding man so dear,
They could not over-reach him or offend.

Long as the sea breathes blessing to thy Town,
 Thou mistress of the Mersey's fruitful tide,
  Let this man's fame be blown toward the West
 And borne back Eastward: let his name abide,
Truth's jewel, in thine uncorrupted crown,
  Hope's star upon thy mighty merchant breast.

William Greenip, the Village Naturalist.

DIED AT KESWICK, NOVEMBER 2ND, 1890.

GOD sometimes fills a poor man's patient heart
With His own reverent love and constant care
For all the things He hath created fair,—
Birds, flowers, the wings that fly, the fins that dart—
And therewithal by Nature's winsome art
Leads him to heights of philosophic air
Where clamour dies, Heaven's ether is so rare,
And bids him walk with gentleness apart.

Friend! such wert thou : the Newlands valley dew,
The star o'er Grisedale's purple head that shone,
Were not more silent, but each stream and glade,
Each bird that flashed, all dusky moths that flew,
All flowers, held commune with thee. Thou art gone.
And Nature mourns the tender heart she made.

Robert Graves, the Village Weaver.

1891.

HERE lies a humble weaver, one who wove
　　Well, till the mill-wheel clacked and clanged no more,
　.Then ate the simple bread God sends his poor,
And ever held it manna from above
Fit for an angel's gathering. Long he strove
　　To help towards Heaven the friends about his door,
　　Versed in his Bible and the holy lore,
They learn, who up the path of duty move.

A Sabbath teacher, teaching line on line;
　　Through him our youth to gentleness were brought
　　　And gentleness learned wisdom: not a child
　　　But as it passed looked up at him and smiled.
　　When Death shall cut our web, may life have wrought
As fair a garment, Robert, as was thine!

Joseph Hawell.

FEBRUARY 20TH, 1891.

GOD has called many following the sheep

    Some to be kings and princes among men,

    And you He called; and Skiddaw's hollow glen

Mourns for its bravest shepherd fallen asleep;

But we who knew you, still your memory keep,

    And at the shearing-time, beside the pen,

    Though gone for ever from our mortal ken,

Your cheery voice will call us up the steep.

For you have climbed the road that leads to Heaven

    The simple road of toil and self denied,

    Of duty done to the far wandering flocks

In dewy cold, hot noons, and stormy even;

    And somewhere He, Whose feet among the rocks

For us were worn, shall lead us to your side.

A. L., Derwent Bank.

JULY 13TH, 1891.

GONE from the flowery bank beside the mere!
No more to feel the purple copses ring
With wild March melody, nor wide to fling
Her casement for the wakening dawn, and hear
The Greta to impetuous Derwent bear
Its music and its mourning. Never Spring
To simpler heart did consolation bring,
Nor Summer brush from tenderer cheek a tear.

For thou didst love the seasons, and thy mind
Was tuned to all the year's vicissitude:
The Spring time bade thee hope, Midsummer
wrought
Large sympathy with being, Autumn brought
Its joy of generous giving to thy mood,
And Winter kept thee hospitably kind.

J. D. Sedding.

IN HOLY TRINITY CHURCH, SLOANE STREET, 1891.

A ROSY pillar 'neath a roof of blue,
  So seemed your soul's upbuilding, then there came
  The wind of Death upon your heart's fierce flame
And passion for the good, the fair, the true;
Your house of life was ashes; but for you
  These roseate pillars and their roof proclaim
  To all who here shall call upon Christ's name,
Death breaks the house, but sets the soul in view.

From noble font and shining pulpit stair,
  From bronze-wrought angels, and rich-carven stone,
  And that dead Saviour gently laid to rest,
  One voice to all the centuries shall attest
That he, who planned this shrine with loyal care,
  Knew, work for God outlived the grave alone.

Mr. J. D. Sedding was engaged on the completion of the
Church of Holy Trinity, Sloane Street, London when in the
spring of 1891 he was suddenly called to his rest.

To the Memory of Oliber Heywood.

MANCHESTER, MARCH 17TH, 1892.

THERE are some lives that never sure should end
  While pain and anguish dwell beneath the sun,
  And heart-ache needs compassion: thine was one,
High-souled and gentle, sympathetic friend!
To thee the city did her sorrow send,
  The poor and fatherless to thee did run,
  All came unto thy mercy's gate, and none
Found thee too full of business to attend.

Now thou art laid beneath the quiet sod,
  The sweetest flowers that ever gladdened sight
    Shall make the silence fragrant o'er thy rest,
    Few mark thy place of slumber, so is best—
  For thy good deeds did ever shun the light;
Done for Christ's sake, known only unto God.

Joe Cape, the Clogger.

FEBRUARY 25TH, 1893.

NO more that veteran figure shall we know,
    Nor hear th' industrious hammer rap and rap,
    Nor see him fashion heel or mould the cap,
And set the beaded nails in shining row,
Nor watch the alder wood to fashion grow
    By knife upon his leathern-aproned lap;
    Death, that doth sometimes come with shoulder-tap,
Smote down the clogger with a cruel blow.

No more his hand will fill the village street
With music of the children's pattering feet,
    But they who follow where his footsteps trod
    Will find that on the mountains never cease
    His song of sweet preparedness and peace,
    Who walked in simple piety with God.

The Gate of Rest.

TO THE MEMORY OF MRS. SARAH THRING AND HER SON,
THEODORE.

SEPTEMBER 26TH, 28TH, 1891.

HER heart was brimmed with full a hundred years
Of patience, wisdom, tenderness and grace,
A hundred years had lined her gentle face
With smile-worn curves and furrowing for tears,
And still forlorn of all her childhood's peers
Quite uncomplainingly she held her place,
And wondered when, to crown her lengthened race,
Would come the wreath that Death in mercy bears.

A hundred years ! a hundred years and one !
She heard a second century's advent chime,
Nor rose to go, she well had learned to wait,
Then to her side God called her eldest son
And both together entered thro' that gate
Where rest is sure—and Life has done with time.

See Note 28.

Elizabeth Atlee.

WIFE OF THE VICAR OF BUTTERMERE, WHO, WHILE ENGAGED
IN MISSION WORK, DIED ON MOUNT OLIVET.

FEBRUARY 7TH, 1892.

Thou did'st not close thine eyes where to the lake
Float forth the cavern-water's echoing tones,
Nor where, snow-white upon the mountain wall,
The great ghyll leaps toward the darkened mere.
No, rather, where scarce audible at all,
The withered Cedron through its yellow stones
Downward its way doth take,
Barren and drear
Among the dead and their ten thousand bones,
Too parched and dry to wake.

Death took thee by the hand,
Not in our mountain land
Where the long sunsets burn
Upon the russet fern,

K

And o'er the vale

The drifts of mountain snow

Fall soft and go;

And down the silent dale

Moves very slow,

With February pale,

The gentle spring,

Bidding the thrush to sing,

Bidding the ravens pair,

And clamour high in air,

Making the shy mole heave

His mountains miniature,

And from her sure retreat

And solitary seat

Commanding love to lure

Our glorious buzzard-king;

The spring that comes to greet

The shepherd on the rock

With dreams of a new flock;

The joyful spring,

With snowdrops at her feet,

And daisies soon to weave

Into a chain and ball ;

The spring that o'er the hills

Will hear the cuckoo call

And by the sounding rills

Keep festival ;

The spring that so makes glad

Each cottage lass and lad

With hope of daffodils.

But thou, thy hand was set

To touch the Master's hem,

To serve thy Lord and Friend

Who some time did ascend

From songless Olivet,

That holy mountain strange

That knows not any change,

Where still the white roads run ·

From shadow into sun,

As in those far off years

When Jesus Christ shed tears

Over Jerusalem.

There where the winter gale

Doth only make more pale

The olive gardens ; there where scarce at all

Come varied seasons, save when now and then

Beyond the city wall,

Ripe figs or berries fall.

And thou wert ripe,

And thou hast heard the word that is the
  best—

"Come unto me, ye weary, and have rest."

Therefore we wipe

Away our tears and say Amen,

For thou did'st go to greet

Thy Lord, and kiss His feet

There where He did ascend ;

And thou hast done His word,

And thou art with thy Lord,
Thy Saviour and thy Friend.

But by sad lake and shore
In this thy dwelling place,
We shall behold thy face
And know thy gentle grace
Not ever more.

A. F.

DIED OF DIPHTHERIA IN THE FEVER HOSPITAL, LONDON, FEBRUARY 24TH, BURIED AT BRATHAY, FEBRUARY 26TH, 1884.

MY grief is such as all men know

Who love and lose an honoured friend ;

My verse shall pay a part I owe,

My debt can never end.

Alice.

FEBRUARY 24TH, 1884.

HER life was as a missal, year by year
Writ in red letters of self-sacrifice,
Illumined quaintly for the children's eyes,
Plain to be read, and musical to hear.
A tale of life so generous, so sincere,
That angels stooped to listen with surprise,
And, for such books are scarce in Paradise,
Bade Death go close it—so they brought it there.

Between the golden chapters week by week,
And 'twixt the lines in ink invisible,
She, skilled in all the arts, but most in this,
Had penned a language only angels speak,
And when their fuller sunlight on it fell,
These words leapt forth in answer—"I am His."

Death the Enlightener.

SOMETIMES for spirits wholly chaste and pure,
   Whose love for truth can know no compromise,
   But still about whose path the mists arise,
Brain-born and soul perplexing, to obscure
The face of Him they long for—Death's great door
   Moves at the hand of One, who satisfies
   Hearts, else for ever hungry, anxious eyes
Whose mortal weakness only Light can cure.

Seeker of Truth and Champion for the Right!
   Thy soul this earth's capacity out-grew,
     Then smiled, and bade us follow; but we mourn,
     For tho' thy voice with cheer beyond the bourne
   Sounds, and shall sound, when thy sweet spirit
     flew,
The dim-lit eyes of many felt the Night.

The Hush of Death.

WHEN through the dark thy spirit all alone
Went to the gate that leads to Heaven or Hell,
But one way led for thee; deep silence fell,
For all the need of ministry was gone;
About thee rose the rushing monotone,
The roar of thousands where ten thousand dwell,
But thou wert guarded by the solemn spell,
The sovereign hush, around Death's awful throne.

And we, with some old story in our ears
Of her who lay in beauty tranced by charm
Thro' days of sorrow and a changing doom—
We moved no hand to wake thee, but in tears
Gazed at thee, saying, "She is safe from harm,"
Then turned—but left our hearts in that still
room.

Vain Regrets.

BITTER when lo! with ashes in his face,
    A friend in passion waves our suit away,
    Or when, the slaves to Time, we cannot stay
For soul-communion any longer space:
But ah! how bitter cruel is the case
    When one we loved, for all we do or pray,
    With ashen face imperious seems to say,
"Belovéd! here no longer love has place."

Then as with hush we close the door and leave
    With what unutterable, dark despair
        For things unsaid, availing deeds undone,
Back to the audience-chamber up the stair
        We needs must turn—but whom we seek is gone—
And in unending loneliness we grieve.

Alice Buried.

FEBRUARY 26TH, 1884.

COLD gleamed the cones of Froswick and Ill Bel,
  And underneath old Fairfields's crown of snow
  Down to the Rotha and the meads below,
The dark-haired woods of stately Rydal fell.
Out shone the sun, the crocus' yellow shell
  Spread starlike, and the daffodils aglow
  Moved in their shrouds, when solemnly and slow
We heard the melancholy mourner's bell.

Sun failed, the cold air shuddered at the sound,
  The Brathay ran unsparkling to the lake,
Sunless we laid her body in the ground,
  But memory made such summer of the spot
  That in our hearts new sunrise seemed to wake,
  And all the valley bloomed forget-me-not.

In Brathay Churchyard.

WE bore her body slowly to the grave
   On royal purple as befits a queen,
  And o'er her pall, with crosses white between,
Were broidered flowers the Lenten season gave,
Gold as her heart was gold. Few words and
    brave
   We said; then laid her where the mosses green
  Made for the wounded earth a gentle screen,
And sang above her sleep by Bratha's wave.

And when the river, golden from the west
   Ran down the purple vale, and Hesperus
    Hung bright o'er Wetherlam, we came to weep,
But in such bridal robes the grave was drest,
   Such gracious flowers looked peacefully at us,
    We well-nigh felt our sorrow share her sleep.

Present but Absent.

I HEAR thy voice by Cumbria's sobbing sea,
   Thy steps are printed in the lonely sand,
  O'er every vale and hill of Westmoreland
Thy gentle form bears company with me.
Most, by Winander's castled shore! with thee
   I seem to hold sweet converse hand in hand,
  On bossy Loughrigg's height at gaze to stand
O'er Langdale's slopes and Bratha's level lea.

The cold March woods will soon with Spring-time
   glow,
  But nevermore thy laughter by the rills
   Will sound, thy feet in prison are so fast;
And tho' thy spirit wanders as it wills,
To thy bright face I cannot look to know
   Which way the angel of the upland passed.

A Sad Communion.

THE prayers went by me in an idle cloud,
  Beneath the altar with fair linen spread
Whereon was holy wine and holy bread,
I seemed to see my sister in her shroud.
Then as in tears I knelt, and kneeling vowed
  The one great oath whereby our souls are fed,
  I heard strange words of comfort from the dead,
And sweet unearthly accents clear and loud.

"Friends! ye who kneeling do remember Him
  Whose voice I followed in the lonely ways,
    Whose eyes I yearned to gaze on—I have found
That there on earth from morn to twilight dim
  They serve him most, who most will serve the
    days
  Whereby the world in brotherhood is bound."

The Haunted Room.

HAUNTED it is by happy, happy days,
   But haunted by the darkest day of all.
The earliest sunbeams from the east that fall
Write one name only with their golden rays.
Her love the silent saffron curtains praise,
   Her name is prinked in pattern on the wall,
   'Alice' the pictures from their places call,
'Alice' the hearth-tongues crackle as they blaze.

The books from off the shelves are strangely moved,
   Or opened lie as if a spirit read,
   Her laughter rings, her silent voice is heard,
We join again in argument she loved—
   The lamp burns low—the fire must needs be
   stirred—
How cold, how dark the room—for she is dead!

L

A Drear Night-Walk.

THE stars are hid, Helvellyn with its snows
  Looms like Carrara's ridge against the moon.
  The sheep call loud as if the time were noon ;
Dogs bark; owls hoot; the wakeful farmyard crows;
Far down the dusky vale the Greta flows
  With wrathful murmur sorely out of tune ;
  We shall not hear its voice of solace soon,
For, hark, the flood to passionate murmur grows.

With sound disordered, hours in disarray
  Alone I walk beneath a starless sky—
    Nay, not alone, Grief holds me by the hand
    And hoarsely whispers, "Thou canst understand
  Now, what large share in earth's full harmony
The loved ones make, the lost ones take away."

Star-Rising.

BUT yester-eve, an eve we cannot know
    Till four more years perplex the calendar,
    I watched the young Moon's silver scimitar
Hang o'er a world of love, that in the glow,
Of yellow sunset hastened from the blow;
    And still fierce Dian in her scythed car
    Pursued, but ever still the beauteous star
Flamed to the hills, to sink unharmed below—

And rise again with splendour: Thou our sun,
    Thou too, tho' Death's pale sword pursuing fast
    Chased momently thy being out of sight,
    Thou hast from that fierce following fled at last,
    And clearer for the coming of the night
Thy radiant round of light and love is run.

𝔥𝔶𝔪𝔫

SUNG AT THE GRAVE OF A. F., BRATHAY CHURCHYARD,
FEBRUARY 26TH, 1884.

HERE beside the Bratha's stream
　　In the Stream of Death we stand—
Bitter waters that would seem
　　To divide us from the land
Where we fain would gathered be,
Sweet, unselfish one, with thee!

Happy soul, with earnest quest
　　For the truth and for the right,
Thou so soon hast entered rest—
　　Thou at length art in the light—
And from clearer heights canst call
Upward! Onward! to us all.

Golden hopes are buried here,

  Precious memories abound,

None more holy, none more dear

  Lie in consecrated ground—

For her grave, when we depart,

Will be found in every heart.

Mourn we all for one whose life,

  Glowing in a world of gloom,

Scattered radiance, softened strife,

  Made for every need some room

In a love that knew no end

To its labour for a friend.

Let the funeral bell be tolled

  Not too sadly: she is bride—

Bride of Death—but we, who hold

  Our dark vigil here, outside,

Know the Master of the Feast

Has received her for His guest.

Though beside the Bratha's stream

   In the stream of death we stand,

These dark waters only seem

   To divide us from the land

Where we all would gathered be,

Happy angel-soul, with thee.

NOTES.

Notes.

Note i. — The society of twelve undergraduate friends, at Cambridge known as "The Apostles"; it included, besides the poet, A. Hallam, Monckton Milnes, Trench, Spedding, Brookfield, Kinglake, Venables, and others.

ERRATA.

Page 103, line 2. Omit "to."

Page 132, line 2. For "S. E. Shawell" read "S. E. at Shawell."

Note 3.—The roof of Coleridge's cottage reminded me of the roof of Somersby Rectory described in *In Memoriam*, ci. The two brothers wrote much of their earliest poetry in the little garret chamber at the northern gable-end of the Lincolnshire parsonage.

"The poplars four that stand beside my father's door" alas! now only whisper in the Laureate's song.

Note 4.—The Shah when last in England summoned Sir Andrew Clark to an audience ; but as he had promised his friend Lord Tennyson, who was somewhat ailing, that he would go down to Aldworth that day, he did not comply with the Shah's request. The Shah was disappointed ; but when he learned that Sir Andrew

Notes.

NOTE 1. — The society of twelve undergraduate friends, at Cambridge known as "The Apostles"; it included, besides the poet, A. Hallam, Monckton Milnes, Trench, Spedding, Brookfield, Kinglake, Venables, and others.

NOTE 2.—Hingvar and Hubba's invasion peopled this part of Lincolnshire with Danes, A.D. 866.

The Dragon of 'Walmsgate' or 'Ormsby,' a village near Somersby, was fabled to have laid waste the neighbouring wold.

It is still remembered in the village how the young boy Tennysons were nearly always seen with a book in their hands as they wandered down the Somersby lanes.

NOTE 3.—The roof of Coleridge's cottage reminded me of the roof of Somersby Rectory described in *In Memoriam*, ci. The two brothers wrote much of their earliest poetry in the little garret chamber at the northern gable-end of the Lincolnshire parsonage.

"The poplars four that stand beside my father's door" alas ! now only whisper in the Laureate's song.

NOTE 4.—The Shah when last in England summoned Sir Andrew Clark to an audience ; but as he had promised his friend Lord Tennyson, who was somewhat ailing, that he would go down to Aldworth that day, he did not comply with the Shah's request. The Shah was disappointed ; but when he learned that Sir Andrew

Clark's absence had been caused by his attendance on his old friend the poet, he gave him, by way of signal honour, the decoration of the "Lion and the Sun." The sonnet is based on the story as sent me by the Laureate.

NOTE 5.—The present Lord Tennyson, in a letter to Sir Arthur Hodgson, of Stratford-on-Avon, says :—

"My father was reading King Lear, Troilus and Cressida, and Cymbeline through the last days of his life. On Wednesday he asked for Shakespeare. I gave him the book, but said—'You must not try to read.' He answered, 'I have opened the book.' I looked at the book at midnight, when I was sitting by him lying dead, on Thursday, and found he had opened it on one of the passages which he called the tenderest in Shakespeare."

NOTE 6.

"29 De Vere Gardens, W., August 5, 1889.

"My dear Tennyson,—To-morrow is your birthday—indeed, a memorable one. Let me say I associate myself with the universal pride of our country in your glory, and in its hope that for many and many a year we may have your very self among us—secure that your poetry will be a wonder and delight to all those appointed to come after. And for my own part, let me further say, I have loved you dearly. May God bless you and yours.

"At no moment from first to last of my acquaintance with your works, or friendship with yourself, have I had any other feeling, expressed or kept silent, than this which an opportunity allows me to utter—that I am, and ever shall be, my dear Tennyson, admiringly and affectionately yours,

"ROBERT BROWNING."

NOTE 7.—I am indebted to the late Charles Tennyson Turner for this reminiscence. On the afternoon of the appearance of their joint first volume of poems Lord Tennyson and his elder brother took carriage, and, driving across the marsh to Mablethorpe, shared their natural triumph with the waves and winds of the wild eastern shore, and came back with shout and song late at night to the moonlit streets of the little market town of Louth.

The late Lord Tennyson, referring to this sonnet, said he had no recollection of the fact which is the motive of it ; but it is fair to his elder brother to reassert that he described the incident as clear in his memory, and that the sonnet was written with his narrative fresh in the writer's ears.

NOTE 8.—All who enter the Memorial Church at Cannes will notice that the emblem of St. George, the English wild rose, has been introduced with beautiful effect into the mosaic of the chancel floor.

NOTE 9.—Herr von Förkenbeck, the chief burgomaster, in reading the address of condolence from the Town Council of Berlin to the Emperor Frederick and the Empress Victoria at the Castle, on Monday, 13th March, 1888, quite broke down ; his voice became choked with tears, whereupon the Empress took the manuscript out of his hand and herself continued the reading of it.

NOTE 10.—The cross was no empty ornament to him; it was the experience of his heart ; it was the confession of his mouth. The Emperor related once how in Königsberg when he was to take the crown from the altar and place it on his head his heart trembled, his hand shrunk back, as it were, from the heavy responsibility attached to the crown, till his eye fell on the crown of thorns of his Heavenly King, and this sight strengthened and encouraged him. (See Dr. Kugel's "Funeral Sermons," as reported in the *Standard* of March 17th, 1888.)

NOTE 11.—Prince Bismarck and Count von Moltke, by special command of the King, were forbidden to risk exposure to the weather during the funeral procession.

NOTE 12.—The benediction was pronounced and the mourners rose to leave ; the funeral march of Chopin pealed forth from the organ ; but before His Royal Highness left the chapel he paused for a moment at the head of his eldest son's coffin, upon which he tenderly placed a small and simple chaplet of flowers. It was from the Princess May.

NOTE 13.—On the morning of Lady Franklin's funeral, I was shown in Noble's studio the bust of Sir John Franklin, now in Westminster Abbey, which he had just completed.

NOTE 14.—Commander Wyatt Rawson was wounded in the Ashantee War at Amoaful. With Captain Nares' expedition to the Arctic, he distinguished himself by giving up his own body's warmth, night after night, in a perilous sledge journey, to keep his frost-bitten comrades alive. He was shot down in the van of the English troops, as he led them through the night, guiding them by the stars, to the attack of Tel-el-Kebir.

The despatch of Sir Garnet Wolseley, dated Cairo, September 24, 1882, runs as follows :—

" Of my Aides-de-Camp I have to regret the loss of Lieutenant Rawson, of the Royal Navy, who was mortally wounded at Tel-el-Kebir. During the many journeys I made by night, I found him of great use in directing our line of march correctly, through his knowledge of the stars. On the 13th instant, I consequently selected him to conduct the Highland Brigade during the night, to the portion of the enemy's works where I explained to him I wished them to storm. This duty he performed with the utmost coolness and success, but lost his life in its execution. No man more gallant fell on that occasion."

NOTE 15.—The pathetic grief upon the faces of the two devoted African servants of Livingstone, Chumah and Susi, who at great personal risk had borne the body of their master from Ilala to the coast, as they stood by the side of the grave in Westminster Abbey, can never be forgotten by those who witnessed it.

NOTE 16.—St. Cuthbert, when a shepherd-boy on the banks of the Leader, saw a vision of angels who appeared to be carrying a soul of exceeding brightness to the heavenly country. He learned afterwards, that at that same time Bishop Aidan of Lindisfarne had passed away, and the boy left his flock and entered the monastic order.

NOTE 17.—This sonnet was written after hearing Dr. Moffat address a great missionary gathering in the Colston Hall at Bristol, September 22nd, 1876. Those who are familiar with this heroic missionary's life will remember the incidents of his adventures with the wild beasts in Bechuanaland which are noticed in the sonnet.

NOTE 18.—Sir R. Anstruther's return after a scrutiny for St. Andrews Burghs.

NOTE 19.—The Archbishop had hardly bid good-bye to Peterborough and entered upon residence at Bishopsthorpe when he died. His body was taken back to Peterborough for interment, within whose cathedral lie the bones of two former Archbishops of York, Aelfric and Kinsius.

NOTE 20.—Longfellow died in the spring of the same year. The resemblance of Rossetti to the traditional portraits of Shakespeare was striking. The last lines of the sonnet refer to the book of poems which Rossetti buried at his wife's death, and was afterwards induced by his friends to take from the tomb and give to the world.

NOTE 21.—I touched on the exquisite loveliness of her little home. " Yes," she said, "but I am never to see a spring here. The three first springs I was at work at the College—and now."—Scott Holland, *Murray's Magazine*, December, 1887.

NOTE 22.—This sonnet was written on hearing that Robert Browning's wish to be buried beside his wife in Florence could not be fulfilled, and that in consequence his body was being brought home for sepulture to England.

NOTE 23.—It is said that in the delirium before his death Lowell seemed to think that he was entertaining Royal guests.

NOTE 24.—Whittier was born at Haver-hill, Massachusetts, on 17th December, 1807. The early years of his life were spent in working upon a farm. After some years of journalistic experience he returned to the farm in 1832. Between 1836 and 1840 he retired to Amesbury and thence forward gave his whole time to literary and poetic work.

NOTE 25.—Through the terrible night of anxiety in the snow-pit on the Dome de Gouter the guides related how Mr. Nettleship kept up their courage and prevented them from falling asleep by constantly singing snatches of song to them. When in his brave desperate attempt to escape on the following morning, the cold and storm overwhelmed him—he stretched out his hands to his guides and speaking to them in a language they could not understand, shook them warmly by the hand, they thought that he thus wished to convey to them that he did not blame them for his death.

NOTE 26.—Mary Stanger, only daughter of William Calvert of Windybrow, and niece of Raisley Calvert, Wordsworth's benefactor, remembered well her going down to Greta Hall to welcome Robert Southey on his return from London after his appointment as Laureate and told me how she helped to weave the crown of laurel which his children then placed upon his head. At her marriage Sara Coleridge and Dora Wordsworth were bridesmaids.

NOTE 27.—Mrs. Harrison of Green Bank or Scale How, Ambleside, was born October 27th, 1801, at Branthwaite, Cumberland. Her father, Richard Wordsworth, an attorney at Whitehaven, was the cousin of the Poet. Dorothy Wordsworth at the death of her father and mother came in 1813 or 1814 to Rydal Mount and was welcomed almost as an elder daughter into the Rydal family, then sadly diminished by the recent deaths of little Catharine and Thomas Wordsworth.

For some six years she remained at the Mount, the third Dorothy beneath her cousin's roof. Afterwards she went to Ulverston, and there married Mr. Benson Harrison of the Lund in 1823.

In 1827 "beautiful Mrs. Harrison," as she was called, came back into the Ambleside neighbourhood and for the next sixty-three years was a gracious presence of active benevolence in the midst of a people who have never forgotten that she was the last of the Rydal Dorothys, and who felt that with her there passed away the strongest tie that still remained to bind them to the Rydal Poet's home.

Truly of her it may be said :—

"That an old age serene and bright
And lovely as a Lapland night
Has led her to the grave."

Her remains were laid to rest in the Ambleside Churchyard on February 25th. The day was a day of cloudless sunshine as brilliant and as warm as a fine May day. The bells of the Church tower had been muffled, and as their six single strokes tolled slowly forth in melancholy cadence, it was almost impossible for the listener not to hear the words they said of sorrowful farewell, "Good-bye, old Friend, good-bye."

NOTE 28.—Mrs. Thring died in her 102nd year; her eldest son died within two days of her, and both were buried on the same day.

END.

GLASGOW: PRINTED AT THE UNIVERSITY PRESS BY ROBERT MACLEHOSE.

BY THE SAME AUTHOR.

18mo, Price 3s. 6d.

SONNETS AT THE ENGLISH LAKES.

Longmans, Green & Co.

Fcap 8vo, Price 3s. 6d.

SONNETS ROUND THE COAST.

Swan Sonnenschein & Co.

Fcap 8vo, Price 5s.

POEMS, BALLADS, AND BUCOLICS.

Macmillan & Co.

Now in preparation.

IDYLLS AND LYRICS OF THE NILE.

SONNETS AT THE SWISS LAKES.